Sabine Fischer, Heiko Pleines (eds.)

The EU and
Central & Eastern Europe

Successes and Failures of Europeanization
in Politics and Society

CHANGING EUROPE

Edited by Dr. Sabine Fischer, Dr. Heiko Pleines and
Prof. Dr. Hans-Henning Schröder

ISSN 1863-8716

Sabine Fischer, Heiko Pleines (eds.)

THE EU AND
CENTRAL & EASTERN EUROPE

Successes and Failures of Europeanization
in Politics and Society

ibidem-Verlag
Stuttgart

Bibliografische Information der Deutschen Nationalbibliothek
Die Deutsche Nationalbibliothek verzeichnet diese Publikation in der
Deutschen Nationalbibliografie; detaillierte bibliografische Daten sind im
Internet über http://dnb.d-nb.de abrufbar.

Bibliographic information published by the Deutsche Nationalbibliothek
Die Deutsche Nationalbibliothek lists this publication in the Deutsche Nationalbibliografie;
detailed bibliographic data are available in the Internet at http://dnb.d-nb.de.

∞

Gedruckt auf alterungsbeständigem, säurefreien Papier
Printed on acid-free paper

ISSN: 1863-8716

ISBN-10: 3-89821-948-8
ISBN-13: 978-3-89821-948-8

© *ibidem*-Verlag
Stuttgart 2009

Contents

List of Tables

List of Figures

Foreword

This book presents a selection of the papers discussed at the Changing Europe Summer School on 'Central and Eastern Europe in a globalized world', held at the University of Bremen, Germany in July/August 2008. The Summer School brought together young academics from all over the world working on issues related to Central and Eastern European societies and the enlarged EU.

Since 2006, the Changing Europe Summer School has each year invited approximately thirty young academics from different disciplines (political science, sociology, history, anthropology, economics, law, geography) to share their work on Central and Eastern Europe. Our main goal is to give them a chance to present and discuss their research projects and become more integrated into the academic community. Participants are selected in an anonymous review process that is kindly supported by the members of our international review panel (for more information on the Changing Europe Summer School see www.changing-europe.de). The results of each Summer School are published in a book series.

It goes without saying that this book would not have been possible without ample support. First of all, our thanks go to the participants in the Summer School, who, with their enthusiasm and knowledge, made it an unforgettable event. We would also like to thank all the referees who supported us in the selection of appropriate participants. We are additionally grateful to all those who helped to organize the Summer School and the book production, namely Hilary Abuhove (language editing), Christopher Gilley (language editing), Judith Janiszewski (style editing), Olivia Koß (Summer School organization), Julia Kusznir (organizational support), Matthias Neumann (technical editing), and Wojciech Rośkiewicz (organizational support).

Last but certainly not least, we want to express our gratitude to the Volkswagen Foundation for its generous support of the Changing Europe Summer Schools.

Bremen and Paris, March 2009
The Editors

Sabine Fischer and Heiko Pleines

Introduction

The changes in post-socialist Central and Eastern European countries have been affected by external influences more than any preceding wave of democratization. Most Central European states quickly and successfully set course for EU and NATO membership, which had major implications for the transformation of their polities, societies and economies. States and societies on the territory of the former Soviet Union and in the Balkans experienced more – as well as more severe – difficulties in their transformation, resulting in a broad spectrum of hybrid political regimes with varying degrees of European integration.

Europeanization is a two-way street. Consequently, the contributions in this book focus on two sets of issues: The first set revolves around the influence of external factors on the transformation processes in Central and Eastern Europe in the context of their relationship with the EU. The second set addresses the ways in which political systems, societies and economies have reacted (and continue to react) to these external forces and how they fit into the European environment.

For the purpose of this book, we use Radaelli's definition of Europeanization, which includes a variety of

> processes of a) construction, b) diffusion and c) institutionalisation of formal and informal rules, procedures, policy paradigms, styles, 'ways of doing things', and shared beliefs and norms which are first defined and consolidated in the EU policy process and then incorporated in the logic of domestic (national and subnational) discourse, political structures and public policies.[1]

The first part of the book deals with Europeanization 'from above', i.e. with the European Commission's deliberate promotion of specific rules, values and related policies during the integration process. Most of the studies conducted in the wake of the EU's eastern enlargement are marked by an inherent selection bias in that they focus almost exclusively on successful processes of Europeanization. By contrast, the contributions in this book include examples of failed Europeanization. The added value of these studies is their demonstration of the shortcomings and limits of Europeanization and of the EU's influence on new and prospective member states.

The contributions in this first part examine five policy fields. Robert Sata looks at minority rights and Suhal Semsit offers a comparative study of migration policies. Noemi Kakucs analyses the politics of gender mainstreaming, while Ingi Iusmen looks

---

1   Radaelli, Claudio M.: Europeanisation. Solution or Problem?, European Integration Online Papers, 2004 (Vol. 8), No. 16, pp. 3–4. An overview of the current state of research is given by Quaglia, Lucia et al.: Europeanization, in: Cini, Michelle (ed.): European Union Politics, 2nd edn, Oxford: Oxford University Press, 2007, pp. 405–420.

at child protection in Romania and Sanin Hasibovic and Manja Nickel jointly examine the governance of domestic violence. The fact that all of these policy fields have a strong normative dimension and address key rights considered part of European identity as defined by the EU allows for direct comparisons. In short, these studies highlight the severe limits of the EU's influence on the national regulation of these policy fields not only in prospective member states but also in countries that joined the EU long ago.

In the second part of the book, the perspective shifts to Europeanization as a process of changing perceptions, values and identities. This process is multi-lateral and much less hegemonic than the implementation of EU-designed policies. It is also much less centred on political actors. Taken together, the contributions in this part illustrate the wide variety of Europeanization effects and underline the necessity of a broader Europeanization approach, as implied in Radaelli's definition. They also provide evidence that the top–down processes described in Europeanization research are sometimes hard to dissect in empirical research. On the contrary, processes of changing perceptions, values and identities related to Europeanization have many directions.

Accordingly, the authors featured in this part contrast the monolithic focus on Europeanization with their observation of an immense variety of societal processes. Raluca Prelipceanu writes on highly-skilled migration in Romania, followed by Elitsa Dimitrova's investigation of Bulgaria's demographic transition. Robert Kulpa analyses Poland's changing sense of self through the prism of queer identity; Anna Wylegała scrutinizes local historical memory in Poland. These authors' contributions show that societal processes are much more complex than the 'common European value system' implicit in the Europeanization approach would suggest.

The third and final part of this book therefore goes beyond the Europeanization approach. It places Europeanization in the context of the various globalization pressures on civil society. The contributions in this part show that Europeanization is – especially in European countries that have not (yet) joined the EU – just one influence among many and often far from the strongest one. Marlene Spoerri takes a look at foreign assistance to Serbia's political parties. Emira Ibrahimpasic examines Muslim women's attempts to exert agency in Bosnia-Herzegovina. Ulla Pape analyses Russian NGOs fighting HIV and Thijs Rommens studies the possible impact of EU policies on democratization in the Southern Caucasus.

The contributions in this volume reflect the wide variety of Europeanization processes taking place in Central and Eastern Europe. They not only serve to illustrate the significant differences among post-socialist transformations, but also highlight the variety of theoretical concepts and methodological approaches at our disposal to research different aspects of Europeanization in the broader context of globalization and identity changes.

Part I. Europeanizations from Above in Post-Socialist EU Member States and Candidate Countries. Case Studies of Success and Failure

Robert Sata

1. The Geopolitics of Minority Politics. Minority Rights under Europeanization in East-Central Europe

The literature of nationalism is not only rich in detailed descriptions of particular ethnic conflicts, but much energy has also devoted to general theorizing about the nature of international minority rights. The relevant literature identifies three main groups of minority rights claims: recognition, participation and self-government. Much of the literature groups together the aforementioned categories of rights claims under the umbrella term of self-determination. I shall also focus our analysis on the principle of self-determination, as employed by international actors, and its relationship to international minority rights. Since international law on minority rights is not entirely clear-cut or monolithic, I shall consider some of the underlying tensions and the main contradictions of competing interpretations in the following pages. Along the way, I will identify the promoted principles and outline the different meanings of the right to self-determination to be found in various international instruments.

The birth of modern international law dates back to the 1648 Peace of Westphalia, which also established the first minority protection system of the international forum. The principle of self-determination is a more recent phenomenon, dating from the American and French revolutions.[1] Religion-based minority rights also dominated the peace treaties of the eighteenth century and the early nineteenth century, but it was the Congress of Vienna that first defined minorities as national groups and not merely religious communities, and also extended the principle of minority rights to these groups.[2]

WWI proved to be an important turning point for minority rights in that the principle of self-determination became an important instrument for the creation of new nation-states or joint-states, mainly in Europe. Given that the borders of existing nations and the newly created states did not fit each other neatly, a set of minority treaties was adopted to safeguard the minorities' right to self-determination.[3] Nevertheless, one can argue that the League of Nations never fully endorsed self-determination as a universal right of the peoples because the treaties it ratified were aimed at protecting certain groups (but not others). In addition, the treaties were applied only to

1   Hannum, Hurst: International Law, in: Motyl, Alexander J.: Encyclopedia of Nationalism, San Diego/CA: Academic Press, 2001, pp. 405–419.
2   Jackson Preece, Jennifer: Minority Rights in Europe. From Westphalia to Helsinki, in: Review of International Studies, 1997 (Vol. 23), No. 1, pp. 75–92.
3   Amstrong, David: From Versailles to Maastricht, London: Palgrave Macmillan, 1996.

the defeated parties of the war or the new states and gave mandates to intervene on behalf of the minorities only to the victors.[4]

Many blamed the minority treaties for the great destruction that took place in WWII; therefore, the United Nations renounced minority rights as such and followed a different trajectory based on the evolution of human rights. Unlike in previous eras, minority rights were considered contrary to international peace and security, and the 1947 Paris Peace Treaties had nothing to say about language or cultural rights. European norms on minority protection evolved in a similar fashion. The European Convention on Human Rights[5] and its Protocols contain no specific provision on minority rights.[6] As such, European norms of minority rights endorsed individual over collective rights and negative over positive rights. In this sense, Europe conformed to the rest of the world, which accepted a principle of sanctity of borders and the territorial integrity of states rather than one promoting the self-determination of peoples.[7]

The most important elements of law-making by European institutions with respect to the internationalization of minority rights are the European Charter for Regional or Minority Languages[8] and the Framework Convention for the Protection of National Minorities[9] (FCPNM). According to the Charter, which was adopted in the spirit of the traditional conception of international minority rights, individuals are the sole bearers of these rights. It lists a wide range of instruments to promote the use of minority languages, but it leaves states with considerable leeway on how to implement them. The Charter protects only the languages themselves, not minority groups. Furthermore, the Charter does not apply to migrant or non-territorial languages and therefore discriminates in favour of historical minorities.[10]

The FCPNM is similar in its conception of minority rights since it does not provide 'clear claimable rights against the state' on the part of minorities.[11] The Convention does not define the subjects of the FCPNM and contains mostly programme-type provisions that allow states discretion in their implementation. The core issues of minority

---

4   Fink, Carole: Minority Rights as an International Question, in: Contemporary European History, 2000 (Vol. 9), No. 3, pp. 385–400.

5   Council of Europe: The European Convention on Human Rights, 4 November 1950, http://www.hri.org/docs/ECHR50.html

6   Medda-Windischer, Roberta: The European Court of Human Rights and Minority Rights, in: European Integration, 2003 (Vol. 25), No. 3, pp. 249–271.

7   Geldenhuys, Deon / Rossouw, Johann: The International Protection of Minority Rights, The FW de Klerk Foundation, 2001.

8   Council of Europe: European Charter for Regional or Minority Languages, 5 November 1992, http://conventions.coe.int/treaty/en/Treaties/Html/148.htm

9   Council of Europe: The Framework Convention for the Protection of National Minorities, 1 February 1995, http://conventions.coe.int/treaty/en/Treaties/Html/157.htm

10   Geldenhuys, Deon / Rossouw, Johann: The International Protection of Minority Rights, The FW de Klerk Foundation, 2001.

11   Deets, Stephen: Reconsidering East European Minority Policy. Liberal Theory and European Norms, in: East European Politics and Societies, 2002 (Vol. 16), No. 1, pp. 30–53, here p. 36.

protection that are explicitly enumerated are: the right to non-discrimination and protection of identity (art. 4, 5 and 6), linguistic rights (art. 10 and 11), educational rights (art. 12 and 13), effective participation and representation (art. 15), and trans-border cooperation (art. 18). The FCPNM also differs from a formal convention in that although it is a binding document, it is not easily enforceable because it is not directly applicable to domestic law but requires interpretation. Its weak wording and escape clauses, together with its deficiencies in the envisioned processes for signing, ratifying and implementing the clauses of the document, enable governments to 'slip through the cracks' with respect to its binding requirements.[12]

Nevertheless, the FCPNM constitutes the most significant development in international minority rights since it is the first multilateral treaty to deal exclusively with these rights that is binding, unlike previous international instruments, which contained only political obligations.[13] Notwithstanding this positive development in international law with regards to minority rights, one must note that although minority rights have been on the EU's foreign policy programme regarding Central and Eastern Europe (CEE), they have rarely made it onto the EU's internal agenda. This has resulted in the criticism that the EU employs double standards vis-à-vis minority rights and lacks an overarching minority policy, which has in turn resulted in very different practices of minority protection in Eastern and Western Europe.[14]

Ongoing Europeanization has been a key concept for the development of minority protection in Europe because the EU has been generating a new type of multi-level governance that challenges the traditional notion of sovereignty. The Pact of Stability has proved to be the most influential instrument of European pressure to settle inter-ethnic relations through bilateral co-operation, linking accession to the EU to the successful settlement of minority issues and also allowing for direct intervention to break deadlock situations.[15] Thus, the Europeanization of minority rights can happen in two ways: the EU as a framework can add new constitutional and policy options to the list

---

12 Gál, Kinga: The Council of Europe Framework Convention for the Protection of National Minorities and its Impact on Central and Eastern Europe, in: Journal on Ethnopolitics and Minority Issues in Europe, 2000 (Winter), pp. 1–17; Troebst, Stefan: The Council of Europe's Framework Convention for the Protection of National Minorities Revisited, in: Speaking About Rights. Canadian Human Rights Foundation Newsletter, 1999 (Vol. 14), No. 2, pp. 10–11.
13 Gilbert, Geoff: Religio-nationalist Minorities and the Development of Minority Rights Law, in: Review of International Studies, 1999 (Vol. 25), pp. 389–410.
14 Amato, Giuliano / Batt, Judy: Minority Rights and EU Enlargement to the East, RSC Policy Paper 98/5, European University Institute, 1998.
15 Bessenyey Williams, Margit: European Integration and Minority Rights. The Case of Hungary and Its Neighbors, in: Linden, Ronald (ed.): Norms and Nannies. The Impact of International Organizations on the Central and East European States, Lanham/MD: Rowman & Littlefield, 2002, pp. 227–258.

of available solutions for disputed issues, and the EU as an active player can also influence the short-term strategies of the parties in conflict.[16]

While EU conditionality is particularly relevant for ethnic accommodation in divided societies, the meaning of Europeanization in terms of minority rights is defined imprecisely. This is true even for the latest initiatives: only limited references to minority protection were present in the 2004 Constitutional Treaty,[17] whose Charter of Fundamental Rights, incorporated into Part II of the Treaty, provides not only for non-discrimination on the basis of 'membership of national minority' but also for 'respect [of] cultural, religious and linguistic diversity' (art. 22).[18] The Europeanization of minority rights also suffers from a lack of clear criteria on which to base minority protection, and because the EU's enforcement mechanisms are poorly developed, the EU often has to rely on other organizations such as the Council of Europe (CoE), the OSCE and NGOs to monitor its own minority policy. More problematic is the fact that there is a lack of genuine social support for the European norms of minority protection; furthermore, the realization and implementation of European minority rights is largely dependent on domestic governments and the political will of those in power.[19]

Promoted international standards have little effect as long as they are considered to be merely normative standards and there is no economic or social policy present to support them. The best encouragement for inter-ethnic co-operation is linking political progress on minority rights to a range of clear political and economic incentives from international institutions.[20] By considering minority protection as a security concern only, the international community has stumbled into the pitfalls of Versailles and

16 Coppieters, Bruno / Noutcheva, Gergana / Tocci, Nathalie / Kovziridze, Tamara / Emerson, Michael / Huysseune, Michel: Europeanization and Secessionist Conflicts. Concepts and Theories, in: Europeanization and Conflict Resolution. Case Studies from the European Periphery, Gent: Academia Press, 2004, available for download from website of Journal of Ethnopolitics and Minority Issues in Europe, 2004, No. 1, http://www.ecmi.de/jemie/download/1-2004Chapter1.pdf
17 Treaty establishing a Constitution for Europe, Official Journal of the European Union, 2004 (Vol. 47), December, C310/01, http://eur-lex.europa.eu/JOHtml.do?uri=OJ:C:2004:310:SOM:en:HTML
18 Cholewinski, Ryszard: Migrants as Minorities. Integration and Inclusion in the Enlarged European Union, in: Journal of Common Market Studies, 2005 (Vol. 43), No. 4, pp. 695–716.
19 Gál, Kinga: The Council of Europe Framework Convention for the Protection of National Minorities and its Impact on Central and Eastern Europe, in: Journal on Ethnopolitics and Minority Issues in Europe, 2000 (Winter), pp. 1–17; Coppieters, Bruno / Noutcheva, Gergana / Tocci, Nathalie / Kovziridze, Tamara / Emerson, Michael / Huysseune, Michel: Europeanization and Secessionist Conflicts. Concepts and Theories, in: Europeanization and Conflict Resolution. Case Studies from the European Periphery, Gent: Academia Press, 2004, available for download from website of Journal of Ethnopolitics and Minority Issues in Europe, 2004, No. 1, http://www.ecmi.de/jemie/download/1-2004Chapter1.pdf; Vermeersch, Peter: EU Enlargement and Minority Right Policies in Central Europe. Explaining Policy Shifts in Czech Republic, Hungary and Poland, in: Journal on Ethnopolitics and Minority Issues in Europe, 2003, No. 1, pp. 1–31.
20 Woodwell, Douglas: Unwelcome Neighbors. Shared Ethnicity and International Conflict During the Cold War, in: International Studies Quarterly, 2004 (Vol. 48), No. 1, pp. 197–223.

the inter-war period, and is reviving the notion of Eastern inferiority. These asymmetric relations between the West and East in turn raise doubts about the genuineness of international commitments to minority protection, which are in fact much weaker than they appear. There is no political desire to question either the Eastern political status quo or Western sovereignty.[21]

***

Let us now examine how European minority rights have affected minority policy and try to outline the role of various international and European institutions and organizations in forging these policies in our selected case studies. We will start with a very brief overview of the Hungarian minority group in Slovakia and Romania, followed by the Russian minority group in Latvia and Estonia. These groups were chosen as case studies by virtue of being two of the most significant minority groups in Central-Eastern Europe. Similarities between Romania and Slovakia on the one hand and Latvia and Estonia on the other will enable us to see the effect of European minority rights in a comparative perspective.

Hungarians have constituted one of the most important minority groups in Europe since 1920, when Hungary effectively lost two-thirds of its population and territory to its neighbours due to the provisions of the Treaty of Trianon that made Romania and Czechoslovakia home to the largest Hungarian minority groups. In the immediate aftermath of the communist regime, Czechoslovakia enjoyed relative ethnic peace because the entire population was preoccupied with establishing the new state. In Romania, while the interim government actively sought ethnic Hungarian support by promising minority protection, clashes between Hungarians and Romanians broke out in the town of Tirgu-Mures very early in March 1990. The situation deteriorated rapidly, with eight people killed and more than three hundred injured before order was restored.[22] Inter-ethnic peace in the region continued to crumble, and after the 1993 split between Slovakia and the Czech Republic, the new Slovak constitution confirmed earlier Hungarian fears of becoming second-class citizens by granting the Slovaks a pre-eminent position starting with its very first slogan – 'We the Slovak People.'[23] Similarly, by late 1991, the Romanian parliament ratified a constitution that pronounced the country a 'sovereign and independent, unitary and indivisible Romanian national state' [art. 1(1)], founded on 'the unity of the Romanian people' [art. 1(4)].[24]

---

21   Chandler, David: The OSCE and the Internationalization of National Minority Rights, in: Cordell, Karl: Ethnicity and Democratization in the New Europe, London: Routledge, 1999, pp. 61–76.
22   Socor, Vladimir: Forces of Old Resurface in Romania. The Ethnic Clashes in Tirgu-Mures, in: Report on Eastern Europe, 1990 (Vol. 1), No. 6, pp. 36–43.
23   The Constitution of the Slovak Republic, http://www.slovensko.com/docs/const/, accessed 13 March 2008.
24   The Constitution of Romania, http://domino.kappa.ro/guvern/constitutia-e.html, accessed 13 March 2008.

At the same time, the Hungarian government, led by József Antall, began to lobby aggressively on behalf of its kin in 1992. Antall refused to normalize relations with his neighbours until they secured the rights of their Hungarian minorities.[25] Hungary also began using its membership in the OSCE to help the Hungarian diaspora, and as a member of the CoE, it threatened to veto its neighbours' admission if they did not institute measures for the protection of minorities immediately.[26] The 1993 Copenhagen Summit of the European Council declared that one of the requirements for membership in the Union was respect for human rights, including minority rights.[27] The signing of friendship and co-operation treaties with neighbours was, and remains, a necessary pre-condition for EU membership. This is why the issue of the Hungarian minority population living outside of Hungary was one of the two original concerns that the Stability Pact was created to address, the other concern being the relations of the Baltic States with Russia.[28]

The High Commissioner for National Minorities (HCNM) was actively involved in trying to ameliorate tensions within Slovakia and Romania as well as between these two states and neighbouring Hungary from 1992 to 1995. In attempting to diffuse these tensions, the HCNM called upon the Romanian and Slovakian governments to take action to combat expressions of ethnic hatred and to provide adequate facilities for national minority language instruction and administrative use. Starting in 1995, the US and NATO also insisted that Hungary settle all its differences with Slovakia and Romania as a prerequisite for membership.[29] In Slovakia, the Meciar government was ousted from office in the spring of 1994, and the new government initiated legislation to comply with CoE and EU recommendations. Doing so only served to foment mistrust between Hungarian and Slovakian co-nationals, however.[30] In the meantime, Hungary also began to curtail its support for Hungarians abroad due to the introduction of the new socialist-liberal government in 1994 under the leadership of Gyula Horn. Horn, unlike Antall, prioritized Hungary's admission to NATO and the EU and concentrated on establishing good relations with Hungary's neighbouring countries.

25 Patkai, Robert J.: Hungarian Minorities in Europe. A Case Study – Ethnicity and Nationalism. A Challenge to the Churches, in: The Ecumenical Review, 1995 (Vol. 47), No. 2, pp. 217–224.
26 Jenne, Erin: Ethnic Bargaining. The Paradox of Minority Empowerment, Ithaca/NY: Cornell University Press, 2007.
27 Stoel, Max van der: The European Architecture of Minority Rights, in: CROSSROADS. The Macedonian Foreign Policy Journal, 2007 (Vol. 1), No. 2, pp. 109–112, http://micnews.com.mk/files/Crossroads%20No%202.pdf
28 Arnould, Michel: Stability Pact. Reassuring Minorities, Guaranteeing Frontiers, in: Forum, 1995, No. 2, pp. 17–19, here p. 18
29 Jenne, Erin: Ethnic Bargaining. The Paradox of Minority Empowerment, Ithaca/NY: Cornell University Press, 2007.
30 Tesser, Lynn M.: The Geopolitics of Tolerance. Minority Rights under EU Expansion in East-Central Europe, in: East European Politics and Societies, 2003 (Vol. 17), No. 3, pp. 483–532.

Yet again, the region saw a major change in ethnic politics with the election of Viktor Orbán's nationalist Fidesz (Alliance of Young Democrats) in Hungary in 1998. Orbán's policies towards ethnic kin abroad were significantly different – whereas Antall refused to normalize relations with Slovakia and Romania due to their treatment of Hungarian minorities, Orbán's government supported Slovakia's accession to the EU and NATO. It was also ready to negotiate with Romania and maintained a dialogue with its neighbours throughout its term.[31] Orbán campaigned on the promise to provide for Hungarians abroad. In 2001, the Hungarian parliament delivered on the promise by adopting the so-called status law, which extended benefits to co-nationals in Slovakia, Romania, Ukraine, Yugoslavia, Croatia and Slovenia – and immediately drew concerns from Hungary's neighbours.[32] The law was severely criticized by international bodies, including the CoE, which argued that the law violated European principles of non-discrimination.[33] Facing this criticism, Hungary started negotiations with Romania and Slovakia – the most vocal critics[34] – and soon curtailed most of the law's benefits.[35] This clearly signalled that Hungary had chosen to champion EU integration over its diaspora's interests.

The preceding pages show that minority policy in both Slovakia and Romania underwent important changes since the regime change, yet simultaneous efforts have also been taken to strengthen national identity in these countries. While Slovakia's minority protection policies formally followed European norms, two pro-Slovak language laws in the 1990s signalled the state's failure to take minority rights seriously and it was only on the basis of a CoE recommendation that laws allowing bilingual locality signs and the formal recording of names in minority languages were passed.[36] Slovakia also signed the 1995 Hungarian-Slovak Friendship Treaty to please Brussels. It was only after Meciar fell from power that Slovakia ratified the European Charter of

---

31   Jenne, Erin: Ethnic Bargaining. The Paradox of Minority Empowerment, Ithaca/NY: Cornell University Press, 2007.
32   Kántor, Zoltán: Nationalizing Minorities and Homeland Politics. The Case of the Hungarians in Romania, in: Trencsényi, Balázs / Petrescu, Dragoş / Petrescu, Christina / Iordachi, Constantin / Kántor, Zoltán (eds): Nation-Building and Contested Identities, Budapest: Regio Books, 2001, pp. 249–274.
33   See European Commission for Democracy through Law (Venice Commission): Preferential Treatment of National Minorities by their Kin-State, adopted by the Venice Commission at its 48th Plenary Meeting, (Venice, 19–20 October 2001), http://www.venice.coe.int/docs/2001/CDL-INF(2001)019-e.asp
34   Ironically, the Slovak parliament adopted a similar benefit law for the 'Slovaks living abroad', offering educational, employment and transportation benefits, based on an ethnic Slovak identification card back in 1997. In 1998, a benefit law adopted in Romania established a budget to grant free higher education in Romania for ethnic Romanians living abroad.
35   Jenne, Erin: Ethnic Bargaining. The Paradox of Minority Empowerment, Ithaca/NY: Cornell University Press, 2007.
36   Tesser, Lynn M.: The Geopolitics of Tolerance. Minority Rights under EU Expansion in East-Central Europe, in: East European Politics and Societies, 2003 (Vol. 17), No. 3, pp. 483–532.

Regional and Minority Languages, and adopted legislation to decentralize administrative competences and establish regional self-government. In Romania, pressure from the EU bodies materialized in the adoption of the Law on Local Public Administration that permitted the use of the minority language as an official language in municipalities with minority populations of 20%. The same pressure led Romania to expand school and university education and allow broadcasting in the Hungarian language after ratifying the European Charter of Regional and Minority Languages.[37] The EU has also influenced Romanian education law; the revised 1997 law granted national minorities the right of education in their mother tongue at all levels from primary to university education.

Russians are the largest ethnic minority in every Baltic State even though their total number decreased by one-third (almost by 600,000) during 1989 to 2000. More than half of the Russians residing in the region (about 700,000) live in Latvia and 350,000 in Estonia.[38] Between the World Wars, Estonian and Latvian societies were ethnically quite homogeneous,[39] but the percentage of the native populations fell drastically in both countries not only because of deportations right after WWII, but also due to the encouraged immigration of ethnic Russians.[40] The collapse of the Soviet Union and the regaining of political independence in Estonia and Latvia cardinally changed social and economic conditions, the directions and intensity of migration and also the ethnic structures of these countries. The level of emigration and repatriation peaked in 1992, when the former Soviet military forces and their family members left the Baltic region.[41]

At the time of Baltic independence, nationality became the key issue of political decision-making and citizenship policies were adopted even before the first democratic elections took place.[42] Having been stripped of their political rights, Russian minorities found themselves in a difficult situation. The Latvian citizenship laws left many of them without the right to vote, to form political parties, or to run in elections.[43] The law granted automatic citizenship only to those with at least one parent who was a citizen

---

37   Brusis, Martin: The European Union and Interethnic Power-sharing Arrangements in Accession Countries, in: Journal on Ethnopolitics and Minority Issues in Europe, 2003, No. 1, pp. 1–21, http://ecmi.de/jemie/download/Focus1-2003_Brusis.pdf
38   Zvidrins, Peteris: Characteristic of the Minorities in Baltic States, http://iussp2005.princeton.edu/download.aspx?submissionId=50900, accessed 15 March 2008.
39   Kirch, Aksel: Estonian Report on Russian Minority, 2001, http://www.ies.ee/kirchrus.pdf
40   Marshall, Monty G. / Jaggers, Keith: Polity IV. Political Regime Characteristics and Transitions, 1800 – 2003, Country Reports, 7 September 2006, http://www.systemicpeace.org/polity/polity06.htm#eur
41   Zvidrins, Peteris: Characteristic of the Minorities in Baltic States, http://iussp2005.princeton.edu/down load.aspx?submissionId=50900, accessed 15 March 2008.
42   See an interesting analysis presented by Smith, David: Russia, Estonia and the Search for a Stable Ethno-Politics, in: Journal of Baltic Studies, 1998 (Vol. 29), No. 1, pp. 3–18.
43   Kelley, Judith: Ethnic Politics in Europe. The Power of Norms and Incentives, Princeton/NJ: Princeton University Press, 2004.

of Latvia prior to 1940, and all others had to satisfy strict criteria.[44] In 1994 a new system for naturalization was introduced that somewhat eased the conditions of receiving citizenship, but only certain age groups could apply each year and applicants had to prove a legal income and knowledge of Latvian history and the Constitution.[45] It was the slow progress of naturalization that caused Latvia to be excluded from accession talks at the end of 1997, and the 1998 amendments to Latvia's citizenship law were by far the clearest indication of the effectiveness of conditionality on imposing minority rights.[46] Yet, the Latvian language barrier remained even in the 1998 amendment of the citizenship law that simplified the language and history tests and granted citizenship to all persons born after independence.

Estonian legislation proved little different: the 1992 Citizenship Law granted automatic citizenship only to pre-1940 citizens and their descendants.[47] Only one out of six Russians could qualify as citizens under this rule, and moreover, a law on aliens was to be adopted in 1993. Its draft stipulated that non-citizens had to renew their residence permits every five years. It was only the intervention of the international forum and at the advice of the HCNM that this stipulation was later deleted.[48] Yet, international intervention only alleviated but did not resolve the tension between the Estonian state and Russian minority. In 1995 the new version of the law increased the residence requirement for citizenship to five years and also introduced further tests that obliged applicants to demonstrate a detailed knowledge of the Estonian Constitution and political system.[49] As a result, the nation-state and democracy were presented as 'conflicting logics' in the aftermath of independence both in Estonia and Latvia.[50]

Similarly, language acts passed in Estonia and Latvia aimed to ensure the superiority of native languages over Russian. While Estonia was a bilingual republic in 1989, by 1995 Russian had become a foreign language and officials were required to prove their proficiency in Estonian. In Latvia, both Latvian and Russian were official languages in 1989; by 1992, non-Latvian speakers were practically excluded from all public positions.[51] Language laws also affected education policy: in Estonia while higher education institutions were required to switch to Estonian by 2000, local government

44 Kolstoe, Paul: Russians in the Former Soviet Republics, London: Hurst, 1995.
45 Kelley, Judith: Ethnic Politics in Europe. The Power of Norms and Incentives, Princeton/NJ: Princeton University Press, 2004.
46 Morris, Helen M.: President, Party and Nationality Policy in Latvia, 1991–1999, in: Europe-Asia Studies, 2004 (Vol. 56), No. 4, pp. 543–569.
47 Ishyama, John: Representational Mechanisms and Ethno-Politics. Evidence from New Democracies in Eastern Europe, in: East European Quarterly, 1999 (Vol. 33), No. 2, pp. 251–266.
48 Kolstoe, Paul: Russians in the Former Soviet Republics, London: Hurst, 1995.
49 Smith, David: Minority Rights, Multiculturalism and EU Enlargement. The Case of Estonia, in: Journal of Ethnopolitics and Minority Issues in Europe, 2003, No. 1, pp. 1–33.
50 Ibid.
51 Karklins, Rasma: Ethnopolitics and Transition to Democracy. The Collapse of the USSR and Latvia, Washington D. C.: Woodrow Wilson Center Press, 1994.

allowed for instruction in Russian in elementary schools; in Latvia there was a gradual move that by 2004 required all state-funded education to take place in Latvian.[52] As such, we could argue that the efforts of the Estonian and Latvian governments suggest that their main goal was to facilitate the spread of the Estonian and Latvian languages through bilingualism in the short run, and a complete language shift in the long run.

State-building policies in the Baltic States drew fierce criticism not only from Russia, but also from international organizations. As a result, the OSCE decided to establish permanent missions in Riga and Tallinn, operating in close co-operation with the HCNM.[53] It was therefore the constant monitoring and diplomatic recommendations, combined with the concerted efforts of European organizations (the OSCE, EU, CoE), that contributed to improving legislature and making both Estonia and Latvia more inclusive. Russian minority organizations, however, also began to display a much greater degree of organization and assertiveness during this period. Minority opposition to proposals that candidates standing in national and local elections should be required to know the Estonian language led to president Lennart Meri's veto.[54] Amendments to Estonian legislation did much to facilitate Estonia's entry into the CoE two years ahead of neighbouring Latvia. However, Russian-speaking parties and organizations continue to reject the current naturalization paradigm in both Estonia and Latvia and they call for an approach based on equal rights.

Russian minority members also lodged several complaints at the European Court of Human Rights (ECHR),[55] which also resulted in beneficial change in state policy. As a result of international involvement, legislation easing the Latvian naturalization law was passed in a referendum in October 1998,[56] Estonia modified its controversial Alien Law[57] and amended the Language Law in April 2000 as recommended by the OSCE.[58] Other international organizations such as the United Nations Development Programme, Delegations of the European Commission and the British Council have done much for Estonian internal societal integration as well as Estonian integration into Europe. The involvement of international actors in ethnic policy-making in the

---

52   Kelley, Judith: Ethnic Politics in Europe. The Power of Norms and Incentives, Princeton/NJ: Princeton University Press, 2004.
53   Laitin, David L.: Identity in Formation. The Russian-Speaking Populations in the Near Abroad, Ithaca/NY: Cornell University Press, 1998.
54   Smith, David: Minority Rights, Multiculturalism and EU Enlargement. The Case of Estonia, in: Journal of Ethnopolitics and Minority Issues in Europe, 2003, No. 1, pp. 1–33.
55   Elsuwege, Peter Van: Russian-Speaking Minorities in Estonia and Latvia. Problems of Integration at the threshold of the European Union, in: European Centre for Minority Issues, Working Paper No. 20, April 2004.
56   Ibid.
57   Spruds, Andris: Minority Issues in the Baltic States in the Context of the NATO Enlargement, http://www.nato.int/acad/fellow/99-01/spruds.pdf, accessed 18 March 2008.
58   Kirch, Aksel: Estonian Report on Russian Minority, 2001, http://www.ies.ee/kirchrus.pdf

Baltics was successful because joining the European Union and NATO was of paramount importance for all of the Baltic States.

***

Our case studies indicate that EU's conditionality had less of an impact in Latvia and Slovakia, while recent signs in Estonia and Romania are a bit more positive in terms of changing attitudes towards minorities. The case studies suggest that three factors influence the effect of European norms of minority protection in forming minority policy in CEE: (1) the extent of domestic opposition to minority protections, (2) authoritarian leaders, and (3) the extent to which ethnic minorities have representatives in government and parliament.[59] While citizenship and minority policy in the region have been liberalized thanks to the involvement of international institutions, simultaneous efforts have also been taken to strengthen national identity. In legal terms, the present minority policy in these countries is entirely consistent with the FCNM. Nevertheless, CEE state-builders have consciously sought to exploit the absence of any universal framework for minority rights, employing the very same arguments that a number of old EU member states had used in order to avoid granting any far-reaching minority rights obligations to their own immigrant populations.[60]

We can conclude that the Copenhagen criteria and the terms of the *acquis communautaire* have provided the EU with a powerful instrument for shaping the process of transition in the prospective member states of CEE. While the future of international minority rights is unsure, I argue that the present international norms of minority rights can be important constitutive norms for future minority protection. Although the rhetoric on Europeanization might suggest otherwise, Europe is not yet 'one'; great inequalities exist and resolving these will be crucial not only for the future of post-communist regions but for Europe as a whole. The greatest promise of European integration is that it makes the prospects of an endeavour bringing true cultural pluralism to Europe brighter than ever before.

---

59   Kelley, Judith: Does Domestic Politics Limit the Influence of External Actors on Ethnic Politics?, in: Human Rights Review, 2003 (Vol. 4), No. 3, pp. 34–54.

60   Smith, David: Minority Rights, Multiculturalism and EU Enlargement. The Case of Estonia, in: Journal of Ethnopolitics and Minority Issues in Europe, 2003, No. 1, pp. 1–33.

Suhal Semsit

2. EU Enlargement Conditionality and the Europeanization of Regulations on the Flow of People. Comparative Analysis of Poland and Turkey Using the External Incentives Model

2.1. Introduction

EU enlargement and Europeanization have been strongly interrelated since the beginning of the fifth EU enlargement process, whose objective was to incorporate the Central and Eastern European countries into the EU. Extending EU membership to these countries has entailed an explicit process of Europeanization, in which there has been a substantial export of *acquis communautaire* to the candidate countries. Without EU enlargement and enlargement conditionality, rule adoption and thus Europeanization would be limited, irregular, slow and weak in these nations.[1]

In the fifth EU enlargement process, Poland, as the largest candidate country in terms of population in Central and Eastern Europe, was high on the EU's agenda regarding the flow of people as well as other policy areas. Poland and its policies on migration are certainly of vital significance with respect to the level of and trends in east-west migrations.[2]

On the other hand, Turkey, which is another country high on the EU's agenda in this matter, started accession negotiations on 3 October 2005. Although the process is still ongoing, negotiations in certain areas were partially suspended in December 2006. In this process, the same conditionality regime has been applied to Turkey as to Poland and other new Member States.[3]

As in other areas, Turkey has been in the process of aligning its policies on the flow of people with those of the EU. The size and challenging nature of the EU *acquis*

---

1   Schimmelfennig, Frank / Sedelmeier, Ulrich: Conclusions. The Impact of the EU on the Accession Countries, in: Schimmelfennig, Frank / Sedelmeier, Ulrich (eds): The Europeanization of Central and Eastern Europe, Ithaca/NY, London: Cornell University Press, 2005, pp. 210–228, here p. 221.
2   Kicinger, Anna: Between Polish Interests and the EU Influence – Polish Migration Policy Development 1989–2004, Central European Forum for Migration Research, Working Paper, No. 9, 2005, p. 3, http://www.cefmr.pan.pl/docs/cefmr_wp_2005-09.pdf
3   Schimmelfennig, Frank / Engert, Stefan / Knobel, Heiko: The Impact of EU Political Conditionality, in: Schimmelfennig, Frank / Sedelmeier, Ulrich (eds): The Europeanization of Central and Eastern Europe, Ithaca/NY, London: Cornell University Press, 2005, pp. 29–50, here p. 41.

in this field makes the alignment process a 'complex' one.[4] Thus, one might expect the issues regarding the flow of people to be one of the most significant and controversial areas in the accession negotiations.

Turkey and Poland, as countries of emigration until recent decades, have gradually been turning into destination and transit countries for migration movements.[5] Both countries will be vested with the primary responsibility for 'guarding' the eastern borders of the EU should Turkey join the EU. Poland, as a transit country, faced some challenges in the Europeanization of its migration policies in the run-up to accession. Thus, Poland has since strengthened its borders as an accession conditionality, and Turkey will be feeling even more pressure to comply with this conditionality in its run-up to accession. In this process, as can be seen in the Polish case, Turkey will also experience the Europeanization process and will need to transform its migration policies to conform to EU conditionality.

Therefore, given the significance and challenging nature of the issue, this article explores the Europeanization process in Turkey and Poland with respect to policy-making on the flow of people as regulated under the Schengen rules in the EU accession process. The extent of EU influence and the limitations of Europeanization in the accession process in these countries will be analysed under the framework of the external incentives model proposed by Schimmelfennig and Sedelmeier[6].

Within this framework, a comparative analysis of Poland and Turkey will be made regarding the process of adopting the accession requirements as stipulated by the Schengen *acquis* on the flow of people, which includes the issues of visa policies, border controls, illegal immigration and the signing of readmission agreements. Policies concerning asylum and the free movement of people exceed the scope of this study.

2.2. Europeanization of the Regulations on the Flow of People in Poland and Turkey under the Framework of the External Incentives Model

In general, the impact of the EU on domestic affairs is called 'Europeanization' in much of the literature on EU studies. As a clear-cut definition, Schimmelfennig and Sedelmeier

---

4   Mitsilegas, Valsamis: The Implementation of the EU Acquis on Illegal Immigration by the Candidate Countries of Central and Eastern Europe. Challenges and Contradictions, in: Journal of Ethnic and Migration Studies, 2002 (Vol. 28), No. 4, pp. 665–682, here p. 678.

5   Iglicka, Krystyna: EU Membership Highlights Poland's Migration Challenges, April 2005, http://www.migrationinformation.org/Profiles/display.cfm?ID=302; Kirisci, Kemal: Turkey. A Transformation from Emigration to Immigration, 2003, http://migrationinformation.org/Profiles/display.cfm?ID=176

6   Schimmelfennig, Frank / Sedelmeier, Ulrich (eds): The Europeanization of Central and Eastern Europe, Ithaca/NY, London: Cornell University Press, 2005.

define Europeanization as 'a process in which states adopt EU rules'[7]. A more detailed definition of Europeanization is

> the reorientation and reshaping of aspects of politics and governance in the domestic arena in ways that reflect the policies, practices and preferences of European level actors.[8]

Radaelli states that Europeanization consists of processes of

> a) construction, b) diffusion and c) institutionalization of formal and informal rules, procedures, policy paradigms, styles, 'ways of doing things' and shared beliefs and norms which are first defined and consolidated in the EU policy process and then incorporated in the logic of domestic (national and subnational) discourse, political structures and public policies.[9]

Conditionality is one of the core components of the Europeanization process. As asserted by the European Commission, 'rigorous but fair conditionality is applied to all candidate and potential candidate countries'[10]. The next stage in the accession process follows depending on the candidate country's progress in complying with the accession requirements.[11] The obligations of the candidate countries include demonstrating the ability to apply the *acquis communautaire*, which consists of over 80,000 pages of legislation.[12]

EU conditionality does not necessarily have the same impact on all candidate countries or policy areas. As an explanatory model for these differing dynamics of EU conditionality, Schimmelfennig and Sedelmeier offer the 'external incentives model'. In this model, the Europeanization process is identified as 'EU-driven' by virtue of its rewards and sanctions, and it is based on the 'logic of consequences' and the 'cost-benefit calculations' of the candidate country. In other words, it can be defined as a 'rationalist bargaining model' in which a candidate country 'adopts EU rules if the benefits of EU rewards exceed the domestic adoption costs'. According to this model, the cost-benefit analysis of the candidate countries is affected by four factors: 'determi-

---

7   Schimmelfennig, Frank / Sedelmeier, Ulrich: Introduction. Conceptualising the Europeanization of Central and Eastern Europe, in: Schimmelfennig, Frank / Sedelmeier, Ulrich (eds): The Europeanization of Central and Eastern Europe, Ithaca/NY, London: Cornell University Press, 2005, pp. 1–29, here pp. 1, 7.

8   Bache, Ian: Europeanization and Britain. Towards Multi-level Governance?, Paper prepared for the EUSA 9th Biennial Conference in Austin, Texas, 31 March – 2 April 2005, p. 3, http://aei.pitt. edu/3158/02/Bache.doc

9   Radaelli, Claudio M.: Europeanization. Solution or problem?, European Integration online Papers (EIoP), 2004 (Vol. 8), No. 16, p. 3, http://eiop.or.at/eiop/texte/2004-016.htm

10   European Commission: Enlargement Strategy and Main Challenges 2006–2007, Brussels, 8 November 2006, p. 5

11   Ibid., p. 5.

12   Schimmelfennig, Frank / Sedelmeier, Ulrich: Introduction. Conceptualising the Europeanization of Central and Eastern Europe, in: Schimmelfennig, Frank / Sedelmeier, Ulrich (eds): The Europeanization of Central and Eastern Europe, Ithaca/NY, London: Cornell University Press, 2005, pp. 1–29, here p. 2.

nacy of conditions', 'size and speed of rewards', 'credibility of conditionality', and 'size of adoption costs'; these factors serve as the determinants for rule adoption.[13]

The external incentives model can be applied to Poland and Turkey with respect to the policy transformation on the flow of people.[14] Before the comparative analysis is conducted, it makes sense to evaluate the main developments in this area in Poland and Turkey in the EU accession process. Concerning the developments in immigration policy in Poland at the beginning of accession negotiations in 1998, the evolution of Polish migration policy mostly depended upon European influences in the framework of EU membership conditionality.[15] However, national preferences, such as the repatriation of ethnic Poles residing in former Soviet countries, also played a role in the evolution of migration policies.[16]

Poland started accession negotiations on Justice and Home Affairs (JHA), also known as Chapter 24, in 2000. As part of the EU's *acquis communautaire*, JHA was the negotiation chapter covering issues such as visa policy, border management, 'illegal' migration and asylum. After the negotiations were completed and it had adopted the Schengen *acquis*, Poland became a member in 2004 despite a number of difficulties.[17] Turkey meanwhile has not yet started the negotiations on Chapter 24 (now called 'Justice, Freedom and Security'). The general tendency in the negotiations is to start with the 'relatively easy' chapters, which stipulate fewer compliance requirements, such as Enterprise and Industrial Policy, Education and Culture, or Science and Research. After the completion of negotiations in previously opened chapters, candidate countries are expected to start negotiations on more comprehensive chapters, such as Chapter 24[18].

At the beginning of the negotiations in Poland on this chapter, a 'policy of Europeanization' existed based on EU conditionality through the channels of screening meetings, accession negotiations and twinning projects. In this process, Polish policymakers began to experience Europeanized policy-making and 'norm diffusion mechanisms'. The common beliefs, ideas and norms of Polish policymakers and the discourse

---

13   Ibid., pp. 2, 8–12.
14   Grabbe, Heather: Regulating the Flow of People Across Europe, in: Schimmelfennig, Frank / Sedelmeier, Ulrich (eds): The Europeanization of Central and Eastern Europe, Ithaca/NY, London: Cornell University Press, 2005, pp. 112–134, here p. 132.
15   Kicinger, Anna: Between Polish Interests and the EU Influence – Polish Migration Policy Development 1989–2004, Central European Forum for Migration Research, Working Paper, No. 9, 2005, p. 28, http://www.cefmr.pan.pl/docs/cefmr_wp_2005-09.pdf
16   Kicinger, Anna / Weinar, Agnieszka / Gorny, Agata: Advanced yet Uneven. The Europeanization of Polish Immigration Policy, in: Faist, Thomas / Ette, Andreas (eds): The Europeanization of National Policies and Politics of Immigration, New York/NY: Palgrave Macmillan, 2007, pp. 181–200, here p. 186.
17   Ibid., p. 181.
18   Economic Development Foundation: Negotiation Process, http://www.ikv.org.tr/en/muzak eresureci.php

on migration issues can be considered as well-Europeanized. On the other hand, institutional Europeanization and the Europeanization of the 'ways of doing things', such as policy-making procedures, is weaker in Poland. Kicinger et al. also emphasize that there has been a lack of lobbies, NGOs and parties interested and participating in the formulation of migration policies.[19] However, Kicinger argues that migration policy in Poland is 'not ideal, not widely discussed, not extremely efficient, not very well articulated and presented and not comprehensive', and is still 'defending Polish interests; not only merely reacting to EU integration requirements.'[20]

Turkey, on the other hand, is still in the early stages of the Europeanization process in migration issues. One could argue that politicians in Turkey consider Europeanization in migration issues as a technical adoption process rather than a comprehensive transformation.[21] Thus, in Turkey, policy Europeanization rather than Europeanization in 'ways of doing things' is mostly expected to take place in this regard, which presents a contrast to the developments observed in the case of Poland.

The major difference between the Europeanization processes in Poland and Turkey in the framework of the external incentives model is the credibility of commitments. The first factor in this model affecting Europeanization is the determinacy of conditions. As shown in Table 2-1 on p. 33, although the determinacy of conditions was low in the case of Poland, it is relatively high in Turkey. The accession requirements on the areas covered in this chapter were not certain in the fifth EU enlargement process because the JHA *acquis* covering these areas was newly developing. This created uncertainty in the candidate countries during those years as they did not know which rules had to be strictly adopted prior to accession. During the accession negotiations on Justice and Home Affairs, it became clear that Poland as well as other candidates were expected to implement the entire Schengen *acquis* before accession. However, this did not mean that the candidates would be immediately included in the Schengen Area upon accession. This aspect certainly affected the cost-benefit analysis made by Polish officials regarding the speed and completeness of compliance, but the benefits of full membership were higher than these costs.[22] On the other hand, since accession

19   Kicinger, Anna / Weinar, Agnieszka / Gorny, Agata: Advanced yet Uneven. The Europeanization of Polish Immigration Policy, in: Faist, Thomas / Ette, Andreas (eds): The Europeanization of National Policies and Politics of Immigration, New York/NY: Palgrave Macmillan, 2007, pp. 181–200, here p. 181–183.

20   Kicinger, Anna: Between Polish Interests and the EU Influence – Polish Migration Policy Development 1989–2004, Central European Forum for Migration Research, Working Paper, 2005, No. 9, p. 28, http://www.cefmr.pan.pl/docs/cefmr_wp_2005-09.pdf

21   Keser, Hasan: Justice and Home Affairs. Europeanization of Turkish Asylum and Immigration Policy in the Light of the Central and Eastern European Experience, in: Ankara Review of European Studies, 2006 (Spring, Vol. 5), No. 3, pp. 115–130, here p. 129.

22   Grabbe, Heather: Regulating the Flow of People Across Europe, in: Schimmelfennig, Frank / Sedelmeier, Ulrich (eds): The Europeanization of Central and Eastern Europe, Ithaca/NY, London: Cornell University Press, 2005, pp. 112–134, here pp. 113–115.

negotiations with Turkey started in 2005, after the big enlargement experience of the EU in 2004, accession conditions were clearer for Turkey despite the continually evolving nature of the EU *acquis* with respect to these matters.

Regarding the second factor, the size and speed of rewards, Poland has had a relatively favourable situation. Although the size of the rewards is the same for each country, i.e. full membership, the speed of delivery has been slower for Turkey due to both 'enlargement fatigue' in the EU and certain political factors. As a result, negotiations on eight chapters came to a standstill in December 2006. This delay negatively affects Turkey's incentives for alignment due to the postponement of the rewards.[23]

When one looks at the size of adoption costs, it is evident that both countries have high adoption costs in migration matters due to their geo-political location and long borders. As asserted by Kicinger et al., the Europeanization of the flow of people is especially critical when it comes to issues such as 'illegal' migration and border management. The size and strictness of adoption costs increased in Poland due to the fear of mass migration from post-Soviet countries in the early 1990s: Poland has a long border with these countries along with a visa-free arrangement with them.[24] Turkey will face the same challenges due to the same issues along with the increasing importance given to border controls.

The last and key factor for Europeanization regarding migration issues in Poland and Turkey is the credibility of conditions. The strong credibility of prospective EU membership is undeniably an essential condition if the EU expects significant domestic change in the candidate country to be achieved.[25] Although Poland had a relatively clearer timeframe for accession, Turkey's time horizon, which was declared as 2014 at the beginning of negotiations, is currently very uncertain due to internal disagreements concerning Turkey's prospective membership. The reluctance of key Member States like France and Germany to grant Turkey full membership as well as the discussions on the 'privileged partnership' alternative to full membership have decreased the credibility of membership for Turkey.[26] Thus, the inconsistency in the EU about conditionality along with contradictory signals from the Member States has created

---

23   Schimmelfennig, Frank / Sedelmeier, Ulrich: Introduction. Conceptualising the Europeanization of Central and Eastern Europe, in: Schimmelfennig, Frank / Sedelmeier, Ulrich (eds): The Europeanization of Central and Eastern Europe, Ithaca/NY, London: Cornell University Press, 2005, pp. 1–29, here p. 13.

24   Kicinger, Anna / Weinar, Agnieszka / Gorny, Agata: Advanced yet Uneven. The Europeanization of Polish Immigration Policy, in: Faist, Thomas / Ette, Andreas (eds): The Europeanization of National Policies and Politics of Immigration, New York/NY: Palgrave Macmillan, 2007, pp. 181–200, here pp. 183–184.

25   Schimmelfennig, Frank: EU Political Accession Conditionality after the 2004 Enlargement. Consistency and Effectiveness, in: Journal of European Public Policy, 2008 (September, Vol. 15), No. 1, pp. 918–937, here pp. 918–919.

26   Ibid., p. 931.

confusion about the promise of full membership.[27] Moreover, the recent stress on 'integration capacity' and the provisions on open-ended negotiations included in the EU's Negotiating Framework for accession negotiations with Turkey, along with the fact that future enlargements may be put to a referendum in France and probably other countries, suggests that Turkey is facing more uncertainty than Poland.[28]

Table 2-1: Table: Factors Affecting the Europeanization Process in Poland and Turkey on the Flow of People under the Framework of the External Incentives Model

	Determinacy of conditions	Size and speed of rewards	Credibility of conditionality	Size of adoption costs	Rule Adoption and European-ization
Poland	Low	High	High	High	High
Turkey	Relatively high	Relatively low	Low	High	Low

Source: Adapted from the External Incentives Model proposed by Schimmelfennig, Frank / Sedelmeier, Ulrich: Introduction. Conceptualising the Europeanization of Central and Eastern Europe, in: Schimmelfennig, Frank / Sedelmeier, Ulrich (eds): The Europeanization of Central and Eastern Europe, Ithaca, London: Cornell University Press, 2005, pp. 1–29, here pp. 12–17.

As shown in the table, the determining factor affecting the difference in rule adoption and Europeanization between Turkey and Poland is the credibility of commitments made by the EU. The increasing uncertainty about the timetable of full membership prospects has further decreased this credibility. This would reduce the degree of Europeanization in Turkey not only in these matters but also in other policy areas, because conditionality cannot succeed without credibility.[29] In the next sections, a detailed analysis of the related matters will be given.

2.3. Alignment with the EU Visa Regime. A Challenge for Relations with Geographically and/or Culturally Close Countries

As one of the post-Warsaw Pact countries, Poland had to change its entire system with respect to the movement of people by introducing more complicated procedures for entry into its territories.[30] By 2004, Poland had ended the visa exemption for

---

27 Schimmelfennig, Frank / Sedelmeier, Ulrich: Introduction. Conceptualising the Europeanization of Central and Eastern Europe, in: Schimmelfennig, Frank / Sedelmeier, Ulrich (eds): The Europeanization of Central and Eastern Europe, Ithaca/NY, London: Cornell University Press, 2005, pp. 1–29, here p. 15.
28 Schimmelfennig, Frank: EU Political Accession Conditionality after the 2004 Enlargement. Consistency and Effectiveness, in: Journal of European Public Policy, 2008 (September, Vol. 15), No. 1, pp. 918–937, here p. 919.
29 Ibid., p. 933.
30 Grabbe, Heather: Regulating the Flow of People Across Europe, in: Schimmelfennig, Frank / Sedelmeier, Ulrich (eds): The Europeanization of Central and Eastern Europe, Ithaca/NY, London:

countries such as Russia, Belarus, Ukraine, Georgia, Kazakhstan, Moldova, Mongolia and Azerbaijan. However, Poland postponed implementing the EU conditionality of imposing visa obligations on Belarus, Russia and Ukraine until the accession in order to reduce the cost of compliance in cultural, economic and political terms.[31] The introduction of new visa regimes with these countries would have created friction between the Europeanization of its domestic politics and the protection of its national interests.[32] In the end, Poland attended to both its national interests and the EU conditionality by liberally issuing visas with no fee for Ukraine citizens.[33]

As part of the accession process, Turkey also will also have to align its visa regime with the EU's positive and negative visa lists. As criticized in the EU's 2008 Regular Report, Turkey still imposes visa requirements on the citizens of sixteen Member States.[34] In addition, there seems to be concerns about Turkey's willingness to align with the EU's negative visa list; Turkey is still reluctant to introduce a visa obligation for Azerbaijan, Mongolia, Uzbekistan, Tajikistan and Turkmenistan.[35] As Kirisci asserts, this alignment process would lead to a tightening of Turkey's visa system, which has been relatively liberal up to now. Kirisci emphasizes that with respect to the Turkic republics, the result could be

> a net cultural, economic, and social loss, as it may resemble the Cold War days when the movement of people between Turkey and these countries was absolutely minimal.[36]

Moreover, this situation would probably fuel irregular migration movements by making it more difficult for people from these countries to come to Turkey. Due to these possible challenges, it seems that Turkish officials will time their actions close to its accession date, just as Polish officials did.

Cornell University Press, 2005, pp. 112–134, here p. 126.

31 European Commission, Poland Scadplus, 2005, p. 5, http://europa.eu/scadplus/leg/en/lvb/e22106. htm; European Commission: Comprehensive Monitoring Report on Poland's Preparations for Membership, 2003, p. 53, http://ec.europa.eu/enlargement/archives/pdf/key_documents/2003/cmr_pl_final_en.pdf

32 Vermeersch, Peter: EU Enlargement and Immigration Policy in Poland and Slovakia, in: Communist and Post-Communist Studies, 2005 (Vol. 38), No. 1, pp. 71–88, here pp. 84, 85.

33 Kicinger, Anna / Weinar, Agnieszka / Gorny, Agata: The Europeanization of Polish Immigration Policy, in: Faist, Thomas / Ette, Andreas (eds): The Europeanization of National Policies and Politics of Immigration, New York/NY: Palgrave Macmillan, 2007, pp. 181–200, here p. 189; Kicinger, Anna: Between Polish Interests and the EU Influence – Polish Migration Policy Development 1989–2004, Central European Forum for Migration Research, Working Paper, 2005, No. 9, p. 19, http://www.cefmr.pan.pl/docs/cefmr_wp_2005-09.pdf

34 European Commission: Turkey 2008 Progress Report, Brussels, 2008, p. 73.

35 European Commission: Turkey 2007 Progress Report, 2007, p. 64, http://www.avrupa.info.tr/Files/File/ab_turkiye_reports/progress-reports-2007-en.pdf; Apap, Joanna / Carrera, Sergio / Kirisci, Kemal: Turkey in the European Area of Freedom, Security and Justice, Centre for European Policy Studies, EU-Turkey Working Papers, 2004 (August), No. 3, pp. 37–41, here p. 29, http://shop.ceps.be/downfree.php?item_id=1145

36 Kirisci, Kemal: Turkey. A Transformation from Emigration to Immigration, 2003, http://www.migrationinformation.org/Feature/display.cfm?ID=176

One way to deal with this delicate issue would be to introduce some flexibility into the visa system on the borders of Poland and Ukraine. Analogously, the same kind of flexibility could be implemented by Turkey to a certain extent after accession takes place.[37]

2.4. Border Management. The Most Costly Adjustment Area

Because the Schengen Area does not have internal borders, the strict management and vigilant 'guarding' of these borders is of the utmost importance in combating 'illegal' migration and organized crime in the developing 'area of freedom, security and justice'[38]. Border management is the most costly implementation area in the Schengen *acquis*, because candidates are supposed to adopt institutional models and working practices so as to establish a new border infrastructure as well as to train vast amounts of officials in border management. The costs are much higher for the candidates that have long borders with non-Member countries. Thus, Poland and Turkey, in addition to the duties expected of other candidates, have to collect data regarding the people crossing their borders and establish the legal machinery to manage asylum claims and refugees. Therefore, Poland and Turkey would be saddled with both the economic and legal responsibility for monitoring and managing the migration movements through the EU's new external borders.[39]

The European Commission has stated that Poland has made important progress in this area despite financial restraints. In 2001, Poland adopted a Schengen Action Plan in order to implement the border management strategy. The significant problems in this process have been a lack of trained staff, limited administrative capacity and weak infrastructure at the borders.[40] The process of Europeanizing border management is ongoing since Poland is currently making preparations to enter the Schengen Area.[41]

---

37   Apap, Joanna / Carrera, Sergio / Kirisci, Kemal: Turkey in the European Area of Freedom, Security and Justice, Centre for European Policy Studies, EU-Turkey Working Papers, 2004 (August), No. 3, pp. 37–41, here pp. 37–41, http://shop.ceps.be/downfree.php?item_id=1145

38   Mitsilegas, Valsamis: The Implementation of the EU Acquis on Illegal Immigration by the Candidate Countries of Central and Eastern Europe. Challenges and Contradictions, in: Journal of Ethnic and Migration Studies, 2002 (Vol. 28), No. 4, pp. 665–682, here p. 665.

39   Grabbe, Heather: Regulating the Flow of People Across Europe, in: Schimmelfennig, Frank / Sedelmeier, Ulrich (eds): The Europeanization of Central and Eastern Europe, Ithaca/NY, London: Cornell University Press, 2005, pp. 112–134, here pp. 118, 123, 126.

40   European Commission: 2002 Regular Report on Poland, Brussels, 9 October 2002, pp. 114–115, http://ec.europa.eu/enlargement/archives/pdf/key_documents/2002/pl_en.pdf; European Commission: Comprehensive Monitoring Report on Poland's Preparations for Membership, 2003, p. 53, http://ec.europa.eu/enlargement/archives/pdf/key_documents/2003/cmr_pl_final_en.pdf

41   Kicinger, Anna / Weinar, Agnieszka / Gorny, Agata: Advanced yet Uneven. The Europeanization of Polish Immigration Policy, in: Faist, Thomas / Ette, Andreas (eds): The Europeanization of

As one can imagine based on Poland's experience, border management would be one of the most challenging and costly issues for Turkey, because it would be responsible for 'guarding' the south-eastern borders of the EU upon achieving full membership.[42] The 2007 Regular Report on Turkey stresses that limited progress has been achieved on external borders and in the Schengen Area. The report emphasized that the National Action Plan on integrated border management

> needs to be equipped with a more precise roadmap containing concrete actions, targets, realistic deadlines, responsible authorities and an estimated budget for each of the actions requiring important investment.

In addition, there have been no tangible steps taken toward the foundation of the new 'border law enforcement authority'. Moreover, the report draws attention to the need for 'training and professionalism of border staff, risk analysis capacity and modernisation of checking equipment.'[43]

Although the borders of candidate countries like Turkey will become EU's external borders after accession, the European Commission has said that candidate countries will have to provide the necessary funds to carry out their border management until accession takes place.[44] Thus, as was seen in the case of Poland, in terms of a cost-benefit calculation, Turkey would have to overcome these financial and institutional costs if it wants to obtain the ultimate reward of full membership.

2.5. 'Illegal' Migration and the Signing of Readmission Agreements

'Illegal' migration has been one of the key issues on the internal agenda of the EU as well as for Turkey–EU and Poland–EU relations since Turkey and Poland are increasingly becoming transit countries for migrants hoping to move to EU countries for a better life.

Actually, thanks to a concerted effort, Turkey has managed to shift transit migration routes to the southern routes of Iraq–Syria–Lebanon and northern routes of Iran–Caucasus–Ukraine, especially in 2000 and 2001.[45] In the decade until 2006, 580,000

National Policies and Politics of Immigration, New York/NY: Palgrave Macmillan, 2007, pp. 181–200, here p. 189.

42   Apap, Joanna / Carrera, Sergio / Kirisci, Kemal: Turkey in the European Area of Freedom, Security and Justice, Centre for European Policy Studies, EU-Turkey Working Papers, 2004 (August), No. 3, pp. 37–41, here p. 41, http://shop.ceps.be/downfree.php?item_id=1145

43   European Commission: Turkey 2007 Progress Report, Brussels, 2007, p. 64, http://www.avrupa.info.tr/Files/File/ab_turkiye_reports/progress-reports-2007-en.pdf

44   European Commission: Issues Arising from Turkey's Membership Perspective, Brussels, 6 October 2004, p. 42, http://ec.europa.eu/comm/enlargement/report_2004/pdf/issues_paper_en.pdf

45   Turkish National Action Plan for the Adoption of the EU Acquis in the Field of Asylum and Migration, 15 March 2005, p. 26, http://www.egm.gov.tr/duyurular/english.zip

'illegal' migrants were apprehended in Turkey. Moreover, 5,500 illegal organizers, including smugglers, were arrested between 1998 and 2006.[46]

The other burning issue in this matter is the signing of readmission agreements by Turkey. In the case of Poland, in 1991 and 1993, Poland signed readmission agreements with the Schengen group of countries and with Germany, respectively, in order to gain visa-free entry to these countries.[47] The agreement started a 'chain reaction' of readmission agreements between Poland and its neighbours and among other EU Member States and Central and Eastern European countries.[48] Polish policymakers strongly believed in the 'irreversible character of the transformation' and therefore recognized these agreements as a 'condition *sine qua non* of the confirmation of Poland's credibility on the international scene.'[49]

In the case of Turkey, the EU officially asked Turkey to sign a readmission agreement with it in March 2003.[50] Due to the concerns of Turkish officials that Turkey would become a 'dumping ground for unwanted immigrants by the EU'[51], a compromise on signing the agreement had not been reached by March 2004,[52] and negotiations began in May 2005.[53]

Actually, Turkey has been waiting for compromises from many countries, and negotiations are underway with many others. These facts show the difficulties the candidate countries face in attempting to convince third countries to sign these agreements. Turkey's declared official policy on this issue is that readmission agreements would be

---

46   Agenda Item 1b. Illegal Migration. Analytical examination of the Acquis, Chapter 24 – Justice, Freedom and Security, Turkey Country session, 13–15 February 2006, pp. 5–6, http://www.abgs. gov.tr/files/tarama/tarama_files/24/SC24DET_ILLEGAL%20MIGRATION%20.pdf

47   Vermeersch, Peter: EU Enlargement and Immigration Policy in Poland and Slovakia, in: Communist and Post-Communist Studies, 2005 (Vol. 38), No. 1, pp. 71–88, here p. 81; Kicinger, Anna / Weinar, Agnieszka / Gorny, Agata: Advanced yet Uneven. The Europeanization of Polish Immigration Policy, in: Faist, Thomas / Ette, Andreas (eds): The Europeanization of National Policies and Politics of Immigration, New York/NY: Palgrave Macmillan, 2007, pp. 181–200, here pp. 184–185.

48   Kicinger, Anna: Between Polish Interests and the EU Influence – Polish Migration Policy Development 1989–2004, Central European Forum for Migration Research, Working Paper, No. 9, 2005, p. 5, http://www.cefmr.pan.pl/docs/cefmr_wp_2005-09.pdf

49   Weinar, Agnieszka: The Polish Experiences of Visa Policy in the context of Securitization, 2006, p. 2, http://www.libertysecurity.org/IMG/doc/The_Polish_experiences_of_visa_policy_in_the_ context_of_securitization-1.doc

50   European Commission: 2003 Regular Report on Turkey's Progress towards Accession, Brussels, 5 November 2003, p. 117, http://ec.europa.eu/comm/enlargement/report_2003/pdf/rr_tk_final. pdf

51   Apap, Joanna / Carrera, Sergio / Kirisci, Kemal: Turkey in the European Area of Freedom, Security and Justice, Centre for European Policy Studies, EU-Turkey Working Papers, 2004 (August), No. 3, pp. 37–41, here p. 22, http://shop.ceps.be/downfree.php?item_id=1145

52   European Commission: 2004 Regular Report on Turkey's Progress Towards Accession, Brussels, 6 October 2004, p. 139, http://ec.europa.eu/comm/enlargement/report_2004/pdf/rr_tr_2004_ en.pdf

53   European Commission: 2005 Regular Report on Turkey's Progress towards Accession, Brussels, 9 November 2005, p. 111, http://ec.europa.eu/comm/enlargement/report_2005/pdf/package/ sec_1426_final_en_progress_report_tr.pdf

signed firstly with source countries, then with transit countries and lastly with destination countries.[54] The last round of negotiations on a readmission agreement between Turkey and the EU was in December 2006. However, as criticized in the 2008 Regular Report, there has been no recent progress in the negotiations.[55]

2.6. Conclusion

When the external incentives model on EU conditionality is applied to policy transformation in the cases of Poland and Turkey regarding the regulations on the flow of people, it is evident that the main difference lies in the credibility of conditionality. In the case of Poland, the economic and political costs of compliance with the Schengen *acquis* were lower than the possible benefits of full membership, which was credible. On the other hand, for Turkey, although the costs of compliance are similar to Poland's, the adoption of the accession requirements is at a low level because of the lack of credibility vis-à-vis obtaining full membership.

Thus, it could be stated that although the costs of compliance is one of the key elements of Europeanization in these matters, the determining variable is the credibility of membership. Therefore, the possible Europeanization of the policies on the flow of people in Turkey in the near future strongly depends on the strengthening of credibility regarding the ultimate reward of full membership.

---

54 Turkish National Action Plan for the Adoption of the EU Acquis in the Field of Asylum and Migration, p. 28, 15 March 2005, http://www.egm.gov.tr/duyurular/english.zip
55 European Commission: Turkey 2008 Progress Report, Brussels, 2008, p. 71.

Noemi Kakucs

3. Contested Global Strategies. Can and Will Gender Mainstreaming Become Local in Hungary?

3.1. Introduction

During the last decade of the twentieth century, gender mainstreaming (hereafter GM) emerged rapidly and spread throughout the world as a new policy approach/strategy/tool aiming to combat gender inequalities. GM is defined as an innovative strategy that requires a radical redefinition of political and policy values and the insertion of gender equality as a fundamental goal in all polices. Besides the UN, the European Union (EU) has become a leading actor in the development of GM as a new policy strategy; however, its gender equality policy was originally shaped within the framework of employment, only later extending to other gender equality issues.[1] The recognition that gender inequalities falling outside the employment context also affect the employability of women and the competitiveness of national economies has pushed the EU to expand its regulations into the area of social policy in order to be able to benchmark the divergent labour market and social policies of the member states.

This chapter aims to explore the way the transfer and institutionalization of GM took place in Hungary, a new member state where the introduction of GM was more a result of external pressure from the EU during accession negotiations rather than that of an internal societal development. The specific goal of this chapter is to find out how GM has been conceptualized by the Hungarian policy makers, which, in turn, has affected its institutionalization and implementation. This is especially relevant, since although the few studies[2] available on the institutionalization of gender equality policies in Hungary offer a detailed description of the institutional and policy developments, they do not offer a discursive analysis that would shed light on the structural and ideological hindrances that obstruct the implementation of gender equality by the actual policy makers. It starts by offering a general theoretical framework on GM

---

1 Walby, Sylvia: The European Union and Gender Equality. Emergent Varieties of Gender Regime, in: Social Politics, 2004 (Vol. 11), No. 1, pp. 4–29; Morgan, Kimberly J.: Towards the Europeanization of Work-Family Policies? The Impact of the EU on Policies for Working Parents, in: Roth, Silke (ed.): Gender Politics in the Expanding European Union. Mobilization, Inclusion, Exclusion, New York/NY, Oxford: Berghahn Books, 2008, pp. 37–59.

2 Open Society Institute: Monitoring the EU Accession Process. Equal Opportunities for Women and Men, Budapest, New York/NY: Open Society Institute, 2002; Krizsán, Andrea / Pap, Eniko: Equal Opportunities for Women and Men. Monitoring Law and Practice in Hungary, Budapest, New York/NY: Open Society Institute and Network Women's Program, 2005; Krizsán, Andrea / Zentai, Violetta: Gender Equality Policy or Gender Mainstreaming, in: Policy Studies, 2006 (Vol. 27), No. 2, pp. 135–151.

with a special focus on the EU context and the enlargement process. The second part of the text presents an analysis of the conceptualizations and institutionalization of GM in Hungary by examining the institutional and policy developments in the field of gender equality, and exploring how the policy makers within this setup see GM and what this means for the implementation of this strategy. For the analysis, two main methods of data collection were used: a content analysis of policy documents, official reports with relevance to GM issued by different institutions and semi-structured interviews[3] with Hungarian public officials employed at various institutions of the state administration at the national and local level, with representatives of women's NGOs and with independent gender experts. However, this analysis can only offer a limited view on the conceptualization of GM in Hungary as the majority of the informants employed in the state administration are public officials involved in the process of dealing with gender equality policies or representative of the civil sector.

3.2. Theorizing Gender Mainstreaming

As GM aims to introduce long-term changes in gender regimes, it requires high level political commitment and comprehensive implementation strategies while the immediate results are not visible. No wonder that the analysis of the process of the institutionalization and implementation of GM has become a great concern for feminist scholars theorizing on its conceptualizations,[4] its scope and methods of implementation,[5] as well as its relation to other approaches to gender equality.[6] Several definitions have

---

3   The interviews were conducted between April and May 2006. Their distribution is as follows: 2 with representatives of women's NGOs (marked A1 and A2); 2 with independent gender experts (D1 and D2); 6 with public officials employed at different institutions of the state administration (B1 from the Ministry of Labour and Employment Policy; B2, B3 and B4 from the Directorate for Gender Equality in the Ministry of Youth, Family and Social Affairs and Equal Opportunities, B5 from the National Development Office, and B6 from the Equal Treatment Authority), and for a comparative dimension, 2 with officials from the local level administration.

4   Bacchi, Carol L.: The Politics of Affirmative Action. Women, Equality and Category Politics, London, Thousand Oaks/CA, New Delhi: Sage, 1997; Bacchi, Carol Lee: Women, Policy and Politics. The Construction of Policy Problems, London, Thousand Oaks/CA, New Delhi: Sage, 2001; Eveline, Joan / Bacchi, Carol: What are We Mainstreaming When We Mainstream Gender?, in: International Feminist Journal of Politics, 2005 (Vol. 7), No. 5, pp. 496–512.; Rees, Teresa: Reflections on the Uneven Development of Gender Mainstreaming in Europe, in: International Feminist Journal of Politics, 2005 (Vol. 7), No. 4, pp. 555–574.

5   Beveridge, Fiona / Nott, Sue / Stephen, Kylie: Mainstreaming and the Engendering of Policymaking. A Means to an End?, in: Journal of European Public Policy, 2000 (Vol. 7), No. 3 (Special Issue), pp. 385–405; Pincus, Ingrid: The Politics of Gender Equality. A Study of Implementation and Non-Implementation in Three Swedish Municipalities, Örebro: Örebro University, 2002; Rubery, Jill: Gender Mainstreaming and Gender Equality in the EU. The Impact of the EU Employment Strategy, in: Industrial Relations Journal, 2002 (Vol. 33), No. 5, pp. 500–522.

6   Bacchi, Carol L.: The Politics of Affirmative Action. Women, Equality and Category Politics, London, Thousand Oaks/CA, New Delhi: Sage, 1997; Bacchi, Carol Lee: Women, Policy and Politics. The Construction of Policy Problems, London, Thousand Oaks/CA, New Delhi: Sage, 2001; Verloo,

been propagated, which might create confusion. Nevertheless, they highlight the difficulty of developing an appropriate definition that could capture all the transformative dimensions of this new approach to gender equality without reifying or omitting anything. However, a crucial problem of the mainstreaming strategy and of gender equality in general lies in their conceptualizations. How can one define gender equality? What does gender (in)equality imply in the Central European and/or Hungarian context? What exactly is to be achieved by GM?

According to the literature, GM was designed to complement the already existing equal opportunity policies and positive action measures by addressing the problem of gender inequality

> at a more structural level, identifying the gender biases in current policies, and addressing the impact of these gender biases in the reproduction of gender inequality.[7]

For its effective implementation several conditions have to be met. Apart from the necessary material conditions like gender budgeting, gender disaggregated statistics and the development of tools for assessment, there is a need for non-material conditions such as political commitment at all levels, influential gender equality machinery, a receptive political atmosphere, etc. Moreover, the literature also highlights the fact that GM is effective only if it is applied by both policy makers and gender experts working together in order to eliminate effectively the unintentional gender bias of seemingly gender-neural policies. Nevertheless, as various case studies at the EU level show,[8] even at the level of EU institutions the implementation of GM remains the task of gender experts alone revealing a technocratic approach to GM and gender issues in general.

3.3. Gender Mainstreaming in the Hungarian Context

GM is a relatively new policy strategy within the EU, with some member states having more inclination towards it than others, and its institutionalization in the EU-15 countries coincided with the processes of Eastern enlargement. Thus the accession of post-socialist CEE countries, which had an experience of gender equality policy

Mieke: Another Velvet Revolution? Gender Mainstreaming and the Politics of Implementation, IWM Working Paper 5/2001, Vienna, 2001, http://www.iiav.nl/epublications/2001/anothervel vetrevolution.pdf

7   Verloo, Mieke: Another Velvet Revolution? Gender mainstreaming and the politics of implementation, IWM Working Paper 5/2001, Vienna, 2001, p. 3, http://www.iiav.nl/epublications/2001/anothervelvetrevolution.pdf

8   See, for instance, Pollack, Mark A. / Hafner-Burton, Emily: Mainstreaming Gender in the European Union, in: Journal of European Public Policy, 2000 (Vol. 7), No. 3 (Special Issue), pp. 432–456; Schmidt, Verena: Gender Mainstreaming – The Institutionalisation of Gender Mainstreaming in the European Commission, Opladen: Barbara Budrich Publishers, 2005; Woodward, Alison: European Gender Mainstreaming. Promises and Pitfalls of Transformative Policy, in: The Review of Policy Research, 2003 (Vol. 20), No. 1, pp. 65–88.

different to the Western European countries, created a challenge to gender equality policies and GM in particular. This is so because (gender) equality policies and GM – in order to be effective – have to be both vertically and horizontally integrated within the post-socialist 'masculinist'[9] democracies struggling with past legacies and neo-liberal demands. The opinion of one of my interviewees (B1), quoted below, rightly captures the ambivalent attitude not only towards GM but also towards gender equality policies in general:

> GM lacks tradition in Hungary as, on the one hand, it is a newly introduced foreign idea, while, on the other hand it is a *socialist escapee* which is over-dimensioned and has to fight for its legitimacy [emphasis added].

As gender equality policies have been introduced under the normative pressure of the EU, the accession countries adopted a minimalist attitude towards it.[10] The low level of political commitment to gender equality policies can be attributed to the dual influence of EU pressure and the legacy of the past. Thus, supra-national pressure for GM can only have a lasting effect if it manages to gain domestic support and/or adapts to local conditions.

Having these aspects in mind, the chapter proceeds with a short overview of the conceptualizations and institutionalization processes of gender equality policy and GM in Hungary by looking at institutional developments in the national machinery, policy documents drafted and adopted under EU guidance, and interviews.

The second half of the 1990s witnessed the re-emergence of national machineries as a requirement of the 1995 *Beijing Declaration and Platform for Action*. As the first step, the gender equality agency, initially called the Secretariat for Women's Policy (to be renamed several times) was established within the Ministry of Labour.[11] Since then, however, any restructuring in the government and each parliamentary election have caused changes in the institutional status of the machinery. The institution was reorganized several times to merge eventually into the equal opportunities apparatus, which included equal opportunity policies formulated with reference to the issues of ethnicity, disability and gender. Consequently, by the beginning of 2006, only one small department was dealing with gender equality issues, while its status in the newly created governmental coalition was not really important and its activities barely visible. Thus, one could assume that in Hungary the re-establishment of the gender equality agency was pursued to satisfy international demands rather than initiatives based in

---

9   Watson, Peggy: Politics, Policy and Identity. EU Eastern Enlargement and East–West Differences, in: Journal of European Public Policy, 2000 (Vol. 7), No. 3 (Special issue), pp. 369–384.

10   Bretherton, Charlotte: Gender Mainstreaming and EU Enlargement. Swimming against the Tide?, in: Journal of European Public Policy, 2001 (Vol. 8), No. 1, pp. 60–81.

11   Krizsán, Andrea / Pap, Eniko: Equal Opportunities for Women and Men. Monitoring Law and Practice in Hungary, Budapest, New York/NY: Open Society Institute and Network Women's Program, 2005.

society. The experience of the gender equality agency being integrated not only into the ministries of labour and employment but also into those of social and family affairs, and of constantly being subject to the whims of the government, shows that gender equality policy is not only narrowly framed in terms of labour and employment as well as family related policies but also lacks legitimacy in Hungarian politics.

During the accession talks, as with other CEE countries, the implementation of EU norms and standards has unfolded through a top–down dynamic and taken the form of highly bureaucratic intergovernmental negotiations. The legal harmonization of the Hungarian legislation with the relevant EU directives, identified by Kirzsán and Zentai as the first stage of the developments in gender equality policy, was followed by a more policy-oriented phase, with Hungary joining various EU level policy processes, which required the introduction of the EU concept and tools.[12] Thus, a complex situation emerged in which GM was pushed from above to be implemented by a government in which there was not a gender equality agency with enough influence on policy to monitor the implementation. This situation also called for increased involvement by societal actors (both academic experts and women's NGOs) to make up for the lack of a proper agency and exert general pressure from below in order to make the GM work. Nevertheless, since according to the underlying principle of GM, the implementation of mainstreaming policy is the task of all policy makers rather than that of a separate institution, let us now proceed with an investigation of how GM is defined by some important policy documents prepared under EU guidance in order to better grasp the overall Hungarian strategy for GM.

As there are no comprehensive policy documents on gender equality or official strategies introducing GM in Hungary, our analysis is limited to some EU documents including the *Joint Inclusion Memorandum*[13] signed in 2003 with the European Commission, the *National Action Plan for Social Inclusion* (2004)[14], as well as the *National Development Plan* (2003)[15]. It does not cover the policy documents issued and published in 2007 in the framework of the European Year of Equal Opportunities for All and the Second National Development Plan (2007).

Before moving to the analysis of these documents, the new legislation on antidiscrimination, the 2003/CXXV Act on Equal Treatment and Promotion of Equal Opportunities should be mentioned. With its adoption in December 2003, Hungary

---

12 Krizsán, Andrea / Zentai, Violetta: Gender Equality Policy or Gender Mainstreaming, in: Policy Studies, 2006 (Vol. 27), No. 2, pp. 135–151.

13 Hungarian Ministry of Health, Social and Family Affairs: Joint Inclusion Memorandum on Social Integration, Budapest: Hungarian Ministry of Health, Social and Family Affairs, 2003.

14 Committee to Combat Social Exclusion: National Action Plan on Social Inclusion. Hungary 2004–2006, Draft, 2004, http://www.icsszem.hu/main.php?folderID=1375&articleID=4961&ctag=articlelist&iid=1

15 Hungarian Government: National Development Plan, Budapest: National development Agency, 2003.

achieved *de jure* fulfilment of all formal legal requirements of regulating discrimination on various grounds. As the Act stipulates, the core element of the Hungarian anti-discrimination policies is to be understood as equal treatment and equal opportunities policies, and gender is considered as one of the many grounds of discrimination. Consequently, all policy documents are prepared in line with this law, which results in a narrow framing of tackling the various forms of discrimination.

The two documents to officially introduce the concept of GM into the Hungarian policy-making context were the *Joint Inclusion Memorandum* (*JIM* 2003) and the *National Action Plan on Social Inclusion* (*NAP* 2004). In both documents, GM is regarded as a horizontal principle and integrated within the larger agenda of social inclusion. A common trend in both documents is that they use the principle of mainstreaming in reference to other disadvantaged groups[16], thus limiting the importance of gender. In contrast to the English versions, GM is understood and translated in the Hungarian documents as equal opportunities for men and women. The two documents reveal a major discrepancy in the Hungarian conceptualization of GM: while the *NAP* (2004) used the term 'mainstreaming' in a general sense referring to the principle of taking into consideration all disadvantaged groups' needs, the *JIM* (2003) employs the concept in reference to the process of creating equal opportunities for women. As a result, although these two documents are supposed to set out the Hungarian GM strategy, neither can be regarded as having a comprehensive approach to it.

Still, within the framework of the social inclusion agenda, another important policy document in Hungary is the *National Development Plan* (*NDP* 2003) prepared in order to make efficient use of the EU structural funds. This document elaborates more on GM. It defines GM to be a horizontal principle,[17] overarching all operational programs. However, only two out of the five operational programs focus as defined in the *NDP* on the need to promote equal opportunities for both men and women. Equal opportunity issues are also discussed in and mainstreaming is put forward by the *Plan* in reference

---

16   Társadalmi Kirekesztés Elleni Bizottság: Nemzeti Cselekvési Terv a Társadalmi Összetartozásért. 2004–2006 Budapest, 2004, p. 21, http://ec.europa.eu/employment_social/soc-prot/soc-incl/nap_incl_2004_hu.pdf. 'Emphasising the principle of mainstreaming in the Hungarian context means that combating poverty and social exclusion is more than a narrowly interpreted task of the social welfare system. Instead, it is an issue of general validity requiring work from all policy areas including all possible levels of administration.' Committee to Combat Social Exclusion: National Action Plan on Social Inclusion. Hungary 2004–2006, Draft, 2004, p. 20, http://www.icsszem.hu/main.php?folderID=1375&articleID=4961&ctag=articlelist&iid=1

17   In accordance with the obligation laid down in Art. 1 of the General Regulation, the National Development Plan strategy defines gender mainstreaming as a horizontal principle which means that the differences between the conditions and needs of women and men should be systematically considered in the process of planning, implementation and evaluation of all measures of the NDP. Hungarian Government: National Development Plan, Budapest: National development Agency, 2003, p. 193.

to other disadvantaged groups – primarily to the Roma and disabled in an attempt to articulate an intersectional approach to the overlapping structures of exclusion.

All the operational programs of the *NDP* (2003) frame the gender inequality primarily as a labour market phenomenon and, by focusing on different sub-groups of unemployed, undereducated, inactive women and young mothers, they represent women as the 'needy' facing social exclusion in need of urgent help. The operational programs emphasize the reconciliation of work and family life, development of childcare facilities, entrepreneurial culture and the role of the social economy. The short- or medium-term implications of such regulations could be regarded as beneficial for women. However, by leaving aside more structural forms of gender inequality (distribution of unpaid work between relatives, stereotyping, etc.) they also demonstrate a narrow understanding of gender equality.

Both the English and Hungarian versions of the *NDP* reveal the same dissimilarities in the general representation of GM as a strategy as in the two previously discussed EU documents. The Hungarian language version of the *NDP* presents a much weaker commitment to any kind of policy measure beyond that of promoting equal opportunities and evades the use of the term 'positive action'. Such shifts in representation and meaning of terminology can be interpreted as a conscious effort aimed at achieving balance between the transnational norms to be adopted and the demands of Hungarian society. Consequently, the policy makers themselves can be considered as veto holders that obstruct the institutionalization of new norms and values. What this means in the case of Hungarian GM is that the miscommunication of gender equality policies shows a compliance with the mainstream societal view of gender politics.

While the policy documents show that GM is understood as securing equal opportunities for men and women, the interviews show varied patterns of conceptualizing GM. The meanings attributed to GM can be grouped as follows: (i) GM as a strategy aimed at creating equal opportunities for men and women, (ii) politically correct definitions of GM, and (iii) definitions that reveal a complete unawareness as far as the meaning of the term is concerned. Nevertheless, only a few of the interviewees highlighted the issue of translation as a determining factor in understanding and implementing GM in Hungary.

The definitions of the first type are as follows: 'the general validation of equal opportunities, and influencing sectoral policies, the two together add up to GM' (B1),

> a strategy aiming to create similar opportunities for women and men … women and men with different social and economic backgrounds should have the same chances … it is a long-term strategy' (A2), and 'a comprehensive conception, which is included in the policy document that deals with EU funding … it is a consistent strategy based on *equal opportunities* for both genders (B5).

As the examples show, there is conceptual confusion about GM among public officials at the national level and the representatives of women's NGOs. However, the public officials at the local level had not even heard of it, and they could not even guess the meaning or explain the terms *gender* and *mainstreaming*. They regarded a separate strategy for achieving gender equality as unnecessary and were instead in favour of propagating equal opportunities policy on other grounds like ethnicity, age, educational and financial background.

In contrast to the unawareness of the officials at local level, the second group of definitions collected displays a thorough knowledge of gender equality policies and GM. Both B2 and D2 defined GM as the 'inclusion of a *gender perspective* in all policy-making and policy-implementation processes at all levels and all stages' (B2) as well as 'from the viewpoint of employees' (D2). As A2 put it:

> The concept as such is not well understood in Hungary. They believe that GM is a project, when it should be a comprehensive principle to be applied in rethinking and re-evaluating all the old and new policies, ... and in all general or action provisions, in policy making and policy implementation, in all spheres of social life the men-women issue is taken into consideration.

The three types of understanding GM correlate to the assumption that there is a division at the level of national government between, on the one hand, public officials in general and the femocrats and individual gender experts on the other. While the public officials interviewed had an unclear understanding of GM, most societal actors and femocrats demonstrated a deep knowledge of the term. Presumably, taking these results into account, one could claim that familiarity with the concept barely extends beyond the group of femocrats, gender experts and some representatives of women's NGOs. This situation implies that the expertise on and the actual execution of GM are radically separated and do not interact during the implementation of the principle at policy-making level.

Furthermore, the conceptual confusion among public officials involved in policy making can also contribute to the mis/translation of the term into equal opportunities policies, as seen in the policy documents. This confusion could be one of the reasons why GM as a principle fails to be included in the actual implementation of *NDP* projects by local governments. The gap between the knowledge of the government level officials, regardless of the inconsistencies, and local level officials also hints to the fact that the effective transfer of gender equality policies and GM from the international level to the domestic level is rather problematic. It seems that international policy directives get stuck somewhere in-between the national and local level, unable to reach the wider public.

During the interviews, the informants' views on the institutionalization of GM were divided as to whether gender issues should be dealt with separately or within the frame of equal opportunities. As mentioned above, the local government officials often argued that women's issues should be a part of a broader agenda of equality politics and not a basis for separate strategy and actions. All the other informants thought of the institutionalization of GM in a highly technocratic and bureaucratic manner. They argued that it should be included in all policy areas, the whole procedure being under the supervision of an influential gender equality agency integrated at government level.

The view that the institutionalization of GM should unfold as a separate institutional mechanism suggests that the very process would provide legitimacy for gender equality policies in general. While B1 argued that the implementation of GM is the responsibility of gender experts at the decision-making level 'who could influence the different departmental policies', both B5 and D2 highlighted the fact that GM

> requires additional effort for all policy makers to think over all policies from a gender perspective, the same with the projects ... additional effort without any visible results (B5).

Since most of my informants were deeply engaged in gender issues, their views on implementing GM in a technocratic manner expressed both their hopes and fears. On the one hand, the process can provide legitimacy to the gender equality strategies, whereas, on the other hand, the inclusion of GM in all policy processes might undermine the need for positive action measures or separate regulations, and ultimately their own positions. From the viewpoint of policy makers less involved with gender issues, the support for a separate institutional mechanism could also be interpreted as resistance to implementation and leaving the task to gender bureaucrats and gender experts.

The duality between the general application of GM by all policy makers and the involvement of experts poses the question of how should GM be institutionalized when the necessary conditions of implementation are not met. Besides this aspect of implementation, the informants also stressed other, sometimes more specific, obstacles hindering the process of GM, such as, for instance, the lack of commitment at the highest political level and the lack of expertise and knowledge. While B1 attributed the failures to the lack of well-trained staff, A2 claimed that public officials

> should regard the equality policy issues more as a field of special expertise and less as an administrative duty; experts should be involved not only in consultation but also in implementation and monitoring.

A successful model of implementing gender equality polices and GM would also require open policy-making processes between governmental departments as well as between the state, social and civic actors[18] to ensure the legitimacy of gender equality issues. The respondents' views on cooperation between the gender equality agency,

---

18 Beveridge, Fiona / Nott, Sue / Stephen, Kylie: Mainstreaming and the Engendering of Policy-making. A Means to an End?, in: Journal of European Public Policy, 2000 (Vol. 7), No. 3 (Special Issue), pp. 385–405.

women's NGOs, and individual gender experts were in many cases contradictory, however. Some informants blamed the national machinery for not collaborating with the women's NGO; some attributed the lack of cooperation to institutional bureaucracy, and others underlined the negative attitude of the Ministry. In contrast, A1 blamed the radicalism and lack of professionalism of some women's NGOs which makes cooperation difficult. As the responses suggest, there is no common view and no consensus on cooperation even among the few individuals (either civil or state actors) who deal with gender issues in Hungary. Contradictions notwithstanding, all interviewees highlighted the need for an umbrella organization embracing all women's organizations that could facilitate the access of women's NGOs to policy.

In conclusion, my informants favoured the institutionalization of GM in a highly bureaucratic and technocratic manner despite the fact that some highlighted the possible threats (such as, for instance, the marginalization of gender equality) and the need for cooperation with women's NGOs. This suggests that gender equality politics lacks political legitimacy, and femocrats, gender experts and women's NGOs wished to restore that legitimacy via the establishment of a strong governmental apparatus, which in turn would legitimate their occupation and institutional existence. The failure to institutionalize GM could be attributed to the staff's low level of expertise in the agency and to the lack of cooperation between state and civil actors. However, the mere fact that GM is translated to equal opportunities both by some of my informants and the policy documents shows that its legitimacy does not depend ultimately on the few employees of an agency lacking in policy access and influence, but on veto holders at higher levels in the state administration.

3.4. Conclusions

GM entered the Hungarian political context only recently as a requirement of the EU legal harmonization process; thus the present situation of gender equality policy and GM in Hungary shows little progress. Until now, Hungary has not adopted any strategic policy document to introduce GM, but has incorporated some elements of gender equality policy from EU documents. The policies adopted are limited in scope with a strong orientation towards the labour market. The term itself has been adopted by the key policy documents, albeit only at formal and rhetorical levels.

It can be argued that the limitations of implementing GM in the Hungarian context stem from the fragmented nature and subordination to equal opportunities politics. The political influence of the Gender Equality Agency is rather marginal and the demand to include the principle of GM in policy making and policy implementation is scarce. Firstly, for GM to unfold effectively in Hungary, several conditions have to be met; among them proper gender budgeting, training and the development of assessment tools can be counted as the very first steps. Secondly, the concept and aims of

GM, as well as the methods and tools of its implementation, should be clarified and developed so that not only gender experts but also policy makers at all levels know what the term means.

Though Hungary is already a member state, it still has much to do in establishing the necessary conditions for introducing an effective GM strategy. As the implementation of GM varies from one EU member state to the next – the concept is vaguely defined and differently understood even within EU institutions – and because EU legislation cannot prevent haphazard implementation at the national level, it is questionable if and how GM will be incorporated into all policy areas at all levels and stages of policy making in the near future.

Ingi Iusmen

4. The Transformation of Child Protection in Romania. Institutions, Instruments and the Dynamics of Change

4.1. Introduction

Human rights conditionality had a significant leverage in changing the human rights protection in Central and East European countries (CEECs) in order to meet the Copenhagen political criteria[1]. Human rights have always been at the heart of European integration, however, the Commission has no internal competence in this field and, furthermore, there is no human rights acquis as such at the EU level.

The transformation of human rights policies in Romania occurred within the context of Eastern enlargement and of the process known as Europeanization East[2], i.e. the impact of the EU's legislative and institutional frameworks on the candidates, and in this case on human rights protection. This chapter examines the transformation[3] of child protection in Romania as part of the EU accession conditionality. The Romanian case study provides unique insight into the EU's accession conditionality – in this case, human rights conditionality – for several reasons. First child protection was an extremely problematic area in Romania and thus the EU leverage on this human rights area is deemed highly significant and far reaching. Second, unlike other Eastern candidate countries, child protection was an accession condition only for Romania. Last but not least, EU's intervention in child protection sheds light on the role of the EU as a norm promoting actor and the more general involvement of the EU with human rights.

This contribution explores several questions related to the transformations underlying child protection in Romania. First, it aims to address the breadth and depth of changes: what were the problems faced by this area and what changes took place

---

1 According to the Copenhagen political criteria, a candidate country has to achieve stability of institutions guaranteeing democracy, the rule of law, human rights and respect for and, protection of minorities, European Council Presidency Conclusions at the European Council in Copenhagen (1993). It should be noted that political criteria of accession – including human rights – are non-negotiable: applicants are supposed to meet the political conditions before the official accession negotiations begin and the EU candidates must ensure that the level of human rights protection meets the EU requirements throughout the negotiation process.

2 For instance, see Grabbe, Heather: The EU's Transformative Power. Europeanisation through Conditionality in Central and Eastern Europe, Palgrave: Palgrave Macmillan, 2005; Schimmelfennig, Frank / Sedelmeier, Ulrich: The Europeanisation of Central and Eastern Europe, London: Cornell University Press, 2005.

3 In this text 'transformation' is primarily understood as the legislative, institutional changes, and at a deeper level, the norms and ways of doing things that had to be adjusted to the EU requirements.

in order to address them? The main foci will be the legislative, institutional changes and the more general normative frameworks that had to adapt to the EU requirements. Secondly, the main instruments and mechanisms underpinning change will be explored – how did those particular changes occur and how effective were those transformations? Thirdly, what are the theoretical models which explain most accurately the level and extent of these changes?

4.2. Child Protection. Problems

The situation of child protection attracted the attention of the Commission from its first Opinion on Romania's Application for Membership (1997): the shortcomings spotted by the Commission and other EU institutions, for instance the European Parliament, were connected both to the organizational framework of child care institutions – still bearing the imprint of the communist childcare institutions – and financial, administrative and legislative problems. The main focus of child protection was the situation of children in residential care or institutions. As the vast majority of institutionalized children were deemed to be adoptable by the system, the crux of the child protection question became the issue of international adoptions. Thus, the importance attached to this human rights area within the political conditionality applied to Romania was great.[4]

4.2.1.   Poor Living Conditions in Old-Style Residential Institutions

First, the situation of the institutionalized children, i.e. children living in state orphanages or institutions, was particularly characterized by poor living conditions, a lack of basic health care[5] and a deplorable material situation. This poor situation in child protection was a legacy of the system for childcare introduced during communism: according to this system, children were abandoned in state orphanages rather than placed in foster homes.[6] The legacy of the communist policy was exacerbated by the failure of the post-1990 governments to reform child protection and to redress the situation. The poor living and material conditions in the large residential institutions led

---

4   For instance, in 2000 Romania's ability to meet the political criteria was dependent on Romania's resolution of the childcare crisis, while in 2004 the accession negotiations came close to a halt at the EP rapporteur's – Baroness Nicholson – suggestion based on the international adoptions question.

5   European Commission: Regular Report on Romania's Progress Towards Accession, 1999 and 2000.

6   'The system introduced in 1970 in an attempt to boost population growth was not accompanied by the requisite machinery for helping birth families for placing children in foster homes; as a result many children were abandoned in squalid state orphanages'; see European Commission: Regular Report on Romania's Progress Towards Accession, 1999, p. 15.

to the so-called 'childcare crisis' in 1999 which made the Commission request that the Romanian government give top priority to child protection.

4.2.2.   Legislative System and International Adoptions

A quick solution to the situation of children in institutions was international adoption. The institutionalization law (11/1990) together with the abandonment law (47/1993) followed by the legislation on adoptions (25/1997) set up the legal framework for the emergence of a Romanian international adoption market which was offer-driven:[7] Romania was a supplier in the activities of agencies specializing in international adoptions. Furthermore, a so-called 'points system'[8] provided adoption NGOs with significant clout in terms of international adoptions. This system prioritized the best interest of adopters and not of children for three reasons: it generated money without putting the interests of the child first; it discouraged domestic adoptions and non-adoptable children were adopted.[9]

From 1990 to 2000, Inter-Country Adoption (ICA) was poorly regulated[10] and it infringed international legislation – namely the United Nations Convention on the Rights of the Child (UNCRC) and Hague Convention on Inter-Country Adoptions – according to which international adoptions were to be seen as a last resort option.[11] However, in the Romanian practice of ICA exactly the opposite was the case: international adoptions had priority over domestic adoptions or the reintegration of children into their families.

Apart from this legislative framework facilitating children's institutionalization via abandonment and thus promoting Inter-Country Adoptions,[12] the entire child pro-

---

7   According to the 'Re-organising the International Adoption and Child Protection System' Report carried out by the Independent Group for International Adoptions, a group of experts set up by the Romanian prime-minister in order to analyse the child protection system in Romania and develop proposals for its improvement, report published in 2002.

8   According to this 'points system' Romanian NGOs received points in return for the provision of services of child protection: thus, on the basis of these points they received children for international adoption.

9   US Report on International Adoptions, 2001, cited in Post, Roelie: Romania. For Export Only, Amsterdam: Eurocomment Diffusion SA, 2007, p. 85.

10   There was no monitoring of or investigation into what happened to all the children who were adopted internationally: thus, a number of 30,000 children were adopted between 1990 and 2004 due to an unregulated system with no post-adoption monitoring (see Nicholson, Emma: Civil Society and the Media in Romania, in: Phinnemore, David (ed.): The EU and Romania. Accession and Beyond, London: Federal Trust, 2006, pp. 64–77, here p. 76).

11   According to the United Nations Convention for the Rights of the Child international adoptions are the last resort, i.e. they come after foster care, institutional care and domestic adoptions (according to Art. 21). Thus, only after all these options are eliminated, can international adoptions be considered.

12   There was a strong correlation between the number of children abandoned and the number of children adopted by foreign families: the more children were abandoned the higher was the demand for children for international adoption. Additionally, this was further reinforced by the

tection system was deeply corrupt: at the heart of the Romanian children's dossier was a true child market.[13] Hence, there was an entire corrupt network supporting the international adoption of children in exchange for money: these were the adoption NGOs and their international counterparts, the Romanian Committee for Adoption, directors of childcare institutions, local judges and the international lobby. Additionally, there was no legal control of the money given for adoption as this was private money and there were no legal instruments to control the money raised through international adoptions.[14]

Furthermore, most of these children were not orphans and hence non-adoptable: they were cared for in institutions due to their families' poverty. Thus, children's parents were bribed to sign the adoption paper so that these children could be declared abandoned and hence suitable for international adoption. In short, the entire system was channelled towards the international adoption of children in exchange for money and as such it violated children's rights as it aimed to provide children for families and not families for children.[15]

4.2.3.   Financial Resources and Administrative Shortages

Financial problems further aggravated the situation of child protection in Romania. In spite of the international financial assistance – provided mainly by the EU, but also by the World Bank, the Council of Europe, etc. – managed by Romanian authorities and NGOs, child protection still suffered from severe lack of funding. According to the Romanian government, the main reason for the childcare crisis and the general poor situation of child protection was twofold: poor management of the available funds and the practice of abandonment caused by poverty. In the same vein, the lack of trained staff[16] and administrative shortcomings in dealing with child protection issues aggravated the Romanian child protection situation.

4.2.4.   Children's Rights and Standards of Protection

The Commission noticed in its evaluation that Romania lacked the necessary standards and legislation to protect children's rights in order to bring the Romanian child protection system in line with the European ones, i.e. UNCRC – which is part of the indirect

---

poor implementation of the law: as there was no counselling provided for mothers – although it was part of the law – the number of abandoned children was high (author's interview with the former secretary of state for the National Authority for the Protection of Child's Rights).

13 Post, Roelie: Romania. For Export Only, Amsterdam: Eurocomment Diffusion SA, 2007, p. 52.
14 Author's interview with the former secretary of state for the National Authority for the Protection of Child's Rights, 10 July 2008.
15 Post, Roelie: Romania. For Export Only, Amsterdam: Eurocomment Diffusion SA, 2007, p. 134.
16 There was a lack of social workers and psychologists also due to the fact that till 1990 the Faculties of Social Assistance and Psychology had been closed by communists.

human rights acquis – and the Member States' practices on child protection. The adjustment of child protection legislation followed a two-stage process: first, Romania had to adopt uniform national standards of child protection; second, the Romanian laws on child welfare had to correspond both to the international and European laws on and standards of child protection.

4.3. EU Instruments and Mechanisms

4.3.1. Financial Assistance

The EU allocated *financial support* via the Phare programme to help Romanian authorities develop modern child welfare services, although there were also other donors – like the United States Agency for International Development (USAID) and World Bank – the EU financial assistance was the most substantial and it was employed for structural reform. The Phare support was substantial and the Commission gradually became involved with how the funding reached its targets.

An important programme supported by Phare was the 'Children First Programme'. This programme focused on the closure of institutions, the creation of alternative services, the improvement of foster care and the contracts for projects given to local authorities, which made them responsible for child welfare. Ultimately, an extensive public information campaign on child protection was funded by the EU.[17] In brief, the Phare programme package involved two key elements: on the one hand, the closure of old-style institutions and the creation of alternative childcare services, and on the other hand, the development of public awareness campaigns. The overall objective was to develop and support the child protection system through supporting the decentralized Romanian authorities.[18]

4.3.2. Twinning

Twinners from the Member States worked alongside Romanian civil servants on child welfare training and measures of child protection. They drafted their own reports on the level of the progress on the ground and made recommendations to the Commission. Furthermore, twinning projects and training were aimed at changing the attitudes of the people working in the system from a collectivist mentality of care to a mentality based on the individual care of the child.[19]

---

17 European Commission: Regular Report on Romania's Progress Towards Accession, 2001.
18 Lessons learnt from Romania. An Assessement of the EU Role and Intervention in the Reform of the Child Protection System in Romania, Transtec report, 2006.
19 Author's interview with the former secretary of state for the National Authority for the Protection of Child's Rights, 10 July 2008.

4.3.3.   Member States' Experts

The Independent Panel of Experts on Family Law was set up in order to advise the Romanian government on the new legislation. From 2003 to 2005, this Panel provided their expertise and know-how in the drafting of the Romanian children's rights legislation. The mechanism of independent experts is employed in cases where there is no detailed Community legislation to act as guidance – as is the case of children's rights legislation.[20] The Romanian legislation needed the Panel's approval before it was passed.

4.3.4.   EU Monitoring and Progress Assessment

The annual Regular Reports drafted by the Commission were crucial monitoring and evaluation instruments. The Commission would provide an objective assessment of the situation on the ground – such as the institutional, administrative or legislative changes – but it also outlined the main shortcomings and made its recommendations in order for Romania to meet the EU accession criteria.[21] The reports acted as instruments in highlighting the Commission's evaluation of the progress in this area and of underlying shortcomings still in place.

4.3.5.   International Instruments

The Commission recommended that Romania adopts some of the international instruments of child protection. For instance, during the ICA crisis Romania became a party to the UN Optional Protocol to the Convention on the Rights of the Child, on the Sale of Children, Child Prostitution and Child Pornography. Moreover, the moratorium was imposed on Romania's international adoption practices due to its failure to respect its obligations under the Hague Convention on Inter-Country Adoptions and UNCRC obligations. In 2004, the Commission concluded that the new legislation met the requirements both of the UNCRC and the practices of the EU Member States.

4.4.   Commission's Recommendations and the Actual Changes

4.4.1.   Reform of the Child Protection System

The Commission's evaluation of the changes in child protection followed the assessment of the situation on the ground, i.e. the main shortcomings of and the latest developments in this policy area, together with its own suggestions and recommendations

---

20   Post, Roelie: Romania. For Export Only, Amsterdam: Eurocomment Diffusion SA, 2007, p. 195.
21   Author's interview with the one of the heads of the former Romania team in the DG Enlargement of the European Commission, 25 May 2008.

in order to redress the underlying problems of child protection. The Commission and the EP's rapporteur Emma Nicholson spoke with one voice and demanded three crucial changes in this area: first, the closure of old-style institutions and creation of alternative services; second, the support of families in order to prevent abandonment; and third, new legislation that should put children's rights and the best interest of the child at the heart of the child protection system.

4.4.1.1. National Standards and Decentralization

In 1998, the Commission welcomed the legislation according to which responsibility for child protection was transferred to the local administration; hence, the *decentralization* of the system had started. One of the core problems identified by the Commission was the lack of *national standards* of care and subsequently the need to a have a single authority responsible for setting those standards and establishing policies related to childcare.[22] Until 2004, the Commission criticized Romania for lacking a uniform set of national standards of child protection: in 2004 national standards for child protection services were adopted.[23] The lack of adequate child protection standards, together with the poor living conditions in the childcare institutions and poorly trained staff escalated in what the Commission called in its 1999 and 2000 reports the 'crisis in childcare institutions', which was mainly due to humanitarian needs.

4.4.1.2. National Strategy

The main problems of the Romanian childcare system were poor living conditions and the lack of basic health care. The Commission recommended in its reports that one way of solving the child protection crisis was both by increasing the financial resources – allocated for this area by the government – and by a better management of the available resources. However, apart from the financial aspect, the Commission recommended[24] that the Romanian government should adopt a *national strategy* on the reform of the childcare system. A National Strategy on the Reform of the Childcare System (2000) had as its basic goals a decrease in the number of institutionalized children and in the number of children at risk of being institutionalized.[25] The Romanian government eventually adopted in 2001 a revised Strategy on the Protection of Children in Need (2001–2004), which had to be implemented at a national level while the reform of child pro-

---

22 European Commission: Regular Report on Romania's Progress Towards Accession, 1999.
23 According to the Regular Report on Romania's Progress Towards Accession, 2004 by the European Commission.
24 Starting with the Commission's Regular Report on Romania's Progress Towards Accession for 2000.
25 European Commission: Regular Report on Romania's Progress Towards Accession, 2000.

tection was closely monitored by the Commission. Despite some initial shortcomings,[26] the Strategy was supported by Phare and it focused on three main issues: the closure of old-style institutions, the de-institutionalization of children and the creation of suitable child protection measures, which was in line with the Commission's requirements from the Romanian government.

4.4.1.3. Closure of Old-Style Institutions and Creation of Alternative Services

The reform of child protection – in order to tackle the poor material situation of childcare institutions – was to be achieved via the closure of large old-style institutions and the adoption of European laws and standards of child protection. One of the key institutional reforms requested by the Commission was the *closure of the old-style institutions* of public care and the *creation of alternative care services*.[27] Also, where possible, children were reintegrated into their natural families. The Commission employed two measures in order to assess progress in child protection. First, a reduction of the number of children in public care, and second, a decrease in the number of residential institutions or their restructuring into family-type modules.[28] The closure of old institutions was accompanied by the development and implementation of modern child protection services, such as family-type modules, day care centres, maternal centres, recuperation centres or foster care networks. In the final report, the Commission approved of the improvements in child protection: a significant reduction in the number of institutionalized children[29] was signalled and the improvement of the living conditions in the remaining institutions.[30]

Additionally, these changes were to be accompanied by greater financial resources allocated to this human rights area. Put simply, what the Commission recommended be put into practice was the following: a reduction in the number of childcare institutions by finding alternative solutions for children living in these institutions – such as

---

26 The Strategy did not fully address – according to the Commission – areas such as the care of young adults leaving the residential care system, the provision of support to families and mothers, and policies to prevent abandonment (see European Commission: Regular Report on Romania's Progress Towards Accession, 2001). This situation was redressed when the new legislation on children's rights entered into force in 2005.
27 European Commission: Regular Report on Romania's Progress Towards Accession, 2000.
28 European Commission: Regular Report on Romania's Progress Towards Accession, 2003.
29 It was also stressed that the term 'institutionalized' children was not synonymous with abandoned children: the children in institutions had parents and families, but these were economically unable to care for them on a full time basis and thus these children were not adoptable. Taking into account this clarification in the meaning of 'institutionalized' children, the number of abandoned children decreased and the number of prospective adoptive families in Romania was higher than the number of adoptable children in 2006 (see Romanian Child Rights Experts Comment on Child Welfare Reform, 2006, http://emmanicholson.info/media/romanian-child-rights-experts-comment-on-child-welfare-reform.html)
30 European Commission: Monitoring report on the state of preparedness for EU membership of Bulgaria and Romania, September 2006.

foster care or services to help families keep their children – standards of child protection, a single authority with clear responsibilities in charge of child protection, better staffing and more financial resources in order to counter administrative and institutional ineffectiveness.

4.4.2. Moratorium on Inter-Country Adoptions

The crux of child protection was *international adoptions*: Romania had to reform its legislation on international adoptions in order to meet European practices on Inter-Country Adoptions. The reform of the child protection system was not deemed possible without this moratorium as international adoptions were detrimental to the reform of the system while the reform of the system meant that Inter-Country Adoptions were not needed.[31]

A High Level Group – made up of the EP's rapporteur on Romania, Baroness Emma Nicholson, representatives of the Romanian government, the Commission, the World Bank, the United Nations Children's Fund (UNICEF) and the World Health Organization (WHO) – was set up in 2001 in order to monitor the measures taken by the Romanian officials in dealing with the international adoptions crisis. A *moratorium* – particularly advocated by the EP's rapporteur – was imposed as a

> mechanism to end practices that were incompatible with Romania's international obligations under the UNCRC and which risked opening opportunities for trafficking in children and other forms of abuse.[32]

The problem of ICA involved both domestic and international actors and it concerned domestic legislative and institutional issues, but international interests – represented by the pro-ICA lobby – were also at stake. Yet, the only way of eradicating the corruption underpinning ICA was by completely banning them.

In spite of the high pressure by the pro-ICA lobby on the Commission and on EP's rapporteur to demand that Romania lifted the ban on ICA, the Commission's formal position on this issue was clear: the EU was not against ICA as such, but against the corruption and bad practices in child protection.[33] The outcome of the ban on ICA was that the number of abandoned children dropped[34] significantly due to two factors: there were no longer financial gains involved, on the one hand, and the development of alternative care services, on the other hand.[35]

---

31 Author's interview with the current secretary of state for the National Authority for the Protection of Child's Rights, 11 July 2008.
32 European Commission: Regular Report on Romania's Progress Towards Accession, 2001, p. 24.
33 Post, Roelie: Romania. For Export Only, Amsterdam: Eurocomment Diffusion SA, 2007, p. 108.
34 For instance, the number of children in institutions dropped from 57,060 (in 2001) to 27,188 (in 2006) according to stats from the National Authority for the Protection of Child's Rights.
35 Author's interview with the former secretary of state for the National Authority for the Protection of Child's Rights, 10 July 2008.

4.4.3. New Legislation on Child's Rights

In 2004 Romania adopted legislation that limited Inter-Country Adoption to extreme exceptions and, according to the Commission, the new rules met the requirements of the UNCRC and the practices of the EU Member States.[36] The ban on ICA was upheld by the new legislation – which entered into force on 1 January 2005 – and it was stated that ICA was no longer a child protection issue due to the new legislation which was deemed to be in line with the European practices.

The new legislation on child's rights and child adoption – law no. 272/2004 and law no. 273/2004 – was highly innovative and it established a legal system of protection that had at its heart the best interest of the child. The 'superior interest of the child' was the core principle that had to be respected during the adoption procedure: this meant that when selecting the adoptive family, aspects related to the cultural, ethnic and linguistic identity of the child would have to be considered. Thus, national adoptions and particularly adoptions from the same geographical area as the child's were the top priority according to the new legislation. Moreover, the child's biological parents – where applicable – had to give their consent for adoption and in accordance with the principle of the child's superior interest, the child's needs, opinions and wishes were to be taken into account when processing adoption.

The new legislation upheld the ban on ICA by providing only one exception for international adoption: when one of the members of the adopting family was the grandparent of the child. Unlike the previous legislation, and crucially important from the EU's perspective, was the fact that the new legislation provided for post-adoption monitoring structures and measures: the Romanian adoption agency which authorized the adoption had to provide information on the development of the child for at least two years. Equally important, and in line with the Hague Convention provisions, Romanian adoption agencies were to prevent any financial gains or other benefits that could result due to ICA: apart from the adoption fee, no other donations or sponsorships were to be received by the institutions processing international adoptions.

Apart from the new legal provisions on ICA, the new legislation addressed the situation of institutionalized children: the new legislation aimed to get most of the children out of institutions and back into their families or place them with foster families and, at the same time, it aimed to prevent infants from entering institutions in the first place. Additionally, a great number of old-style residential institutions were closed. All these aspects brought the Romanian legislation on child protection and ICA in line with the EU requirements: the Romanian legislation on child's rights was

---

36   European Commission: Regular Report on Romania's Progress Towards Accession, 2004.

recommended as a model that was in many ways interesting and revolutionary even for some Western European states.[37]

The actual implementation of the newly adopted rules and laws was the main concern of the Commission in its final reports. The new legislation started to bear fruit by mid-2005 and significant progress was achieved. Alternative childcare services were further created, i.e. children were placed with foster parents, and the number of abandoned children started to decrease.[38] Prior to accession, there were new legislative and institutional structures in place for child protection, which highlighted positive prospects for child protection after the accession. The backbone of the new legislation was the prevention of abandonment by targeting the families at risk and by making institutional care the last option of child protection.

The new legislation together with the reform of child protection meant that the entire Romanian child protection system had to be redesigned: the focus of the system shifted from institutional care to family care, with significant emphasis being put on the prevention of child abandonment – and hence institutionalization – and on the provision of new community services, such as foster care or the return of the child to its natural family.

4.4.4. The National Authority for the Protection of Child's Rights

The National Authority for the Protection of Child's Rights (NAPCR) was created in 1997 and it played a crucial role as the main governmental body in charge of the implementation of child protection reform. The main role of the NAPCR is to provide the protection of child's rights by direct coordination of the General Directions of Social Assistance and Child Protection – the agencies in charge with child protection at the local level – and by influencing those policies on health, education or justice that might have an impact on children's rights.[39]

4.4.5. 'Still Work to Do'

Despite the radical overhaul of the Romanian child protection system – the reform, new legislation, institutions and alternative care services – there is still work to do in this area. Although it is an exportable model – especially to other CEECs – the

---

37 For instance, some of the European states do not have legal provisions on the punishment of the violence against children and the Romanian legislation took into account the latest conventions on child's rights, such as the Convention on Contact concerning Children (part of the Council of Europe) if the parents are separated or divorced (author's interview with the state secretary of child protection).

38 Romanian Child Rights Experts Comment on Child Welfare Reform, 2006, http://emmanichol son.info/media/romanian-child-rights-experts-comment-on-child-welfare-reform.html

39 Author's interview with the current secretary of state for the National Authority for the Protection of Child's Rights, 11 July 2008.

Romanian child protection system is faced with several problems. First, the development of diverse services should continue in order to address new situations, such as parents' migration and children being left to live with relatives or grandparents.[40] Second, there is still work to be done on the professionalism of those working in the system. More training is needed and, above all, there should be more staff that has a vocation for working with children.[41] Third, the authorities dealing with children – either in health or education – should be more familiar with child's rights and the international conventions in this area.[42] Last but not least, there ought to be created Children's Tribunals where children's rights should be defended in case children are brought before a court of justice.[43]

4.4.6.   Theoretical Models

There are two theoretical models that explain change due to Europeanization: rationalist and sociological models of change. While rationalist approaches focus on the utility-based, i.e. cost-benefit, dimension of change, the constructivist or socialization approaches describes the ideational and norm internalization aspects of change. Rationalist approaches describe a material pattern of change: the transformation of human rights policies and hence compliance with EU requirements impose material costs at the domestic level. However, transformation occurs if domestic costs are lower than the benefits of transformation, or if, in the long term, the incentives of transformation outweigh the short term costs of change. Conversely, transformation – according to the sociological framework – occurs when norm internalization and social learning are evinced between the supranational and national levels.

The transformation of child protection in Romanian neatly fits within a rationalist model, or what is described as the external incentives model of rule transfer[44]. The EU accession conditionality meant that Romania had to reform its child protection system in order to meet the EU conditions and thus join the EU. Thus, the main carrot was EU membership, while the sticks – i.e. the costs underlying the whole process of reform and change – in spite of their shortcomings, were perceived as less significant in the long run if compared with the benefits of membership. A cost-benefit analysis demonstrates that the costs of the system overhaul were outweighed by the

---

40   Author's interview with the former secretary of state for the National Authority for the Protection of Child's Rights, 10 July 2008.
41   Author's interview with the current secretary of state for the National Authority for the Protection of Child's Rights, 11 July 2008.
42   Author's interview with the former secretary of state for the National Authority for the Protection of Child's Rights, 10 July 2008.
43   Ibid.
44   Schimmelfennig, Franck / Sedelmeier, Ulrich: Governance by Conditionality. EU Rule Transfer to the Candidate Countries of Central and Eastern Europe, in: Journal of European Public Policy, 2004 (Vol. 11), No. 4, pp. 661–679.

benefit of EU membership – the main incentive for change – but additionally, transformation was less costly also due to the EU's substantial financial and technical support prior to accession.

Processes of social learning and ways of doing things also accompanied the changes in child protection. This was particularly due to EU twinning and the role of EU experts in transferring the know-how and normative approach to children's rights. As shown above, there was an extensive learning process which amounted to a shift in attitudes, procedures, and modes of care of those working in the system with regard to children care.[45] This theoretical framework is in line with Checkel's[46] view that rationalist models and sociological processes of learning should be seen as complementary rather than as opposite explanations.

4.5. Conclusion

This chapter examined the role played by the EU in transforming child protection legislation and institutions in Romania. The EU had a great impact in forging the overhaul of the Romanian child protection system. However, EU's involvement with child's rights in Romania has implications not only for the theory and practice of child protection in Romania, but also for the role and effectiveness of the EU as a human rights promoter in areas, like children's rights, which are not EU issues per se.

---

45 Author's interview with the former secretary of state for the National Authority for the Protection of Child's Rights, 10 July 2008.

46 Checkel, Jeffrey T. (ed.): International Institutions and Socialization in Europe, Cambridge: Cambridge University Press, 2007.

Sanin Hasibovic and Manja Nickel

5. Governance of Domestic Violence in Central and South-Eastern Europe

5.1. Introduction

In the last two decades Central and South East European (CSEE) countries have been characterized by processes of state- and nation-building, political and economic transitions, ever-growing social heterogeneity, and increasing integration into the world and European Community. It is well established that these transformation processes are deeply entangled with gender relations. Yet gender relations are not only an object of system changes, but are also resources of social, cultural and political transition. They are part of in-group and out-group differentiation in nation-building processes, involving education and socialization, the reconstruction of social institutions such as the family, and the political culture of the individual country.[1] Thus, to understand transformation processes in CSEE in a comprehensive way, the analysis of gender relations is indispensable. We assume that issues of culture and gender relations constitute important frames and resources in democratization processes as well as in the political efforts to achieve membership in the European Union. At present, the governance of cultural and gender differences (e.g. the recognition of minorities and the anti-discrimination of women) is a relevant issue in accession talks with the EU.

In this general context, we are concerned in this chapter with the socially contested issue of domestic violence. The problem of domestic, especially gender-based, violence has sparked a vivid debate in various European countries on gender relations, cultural patterns, the role of tradition, patriarchy, etc. Special focus has been placed upon the governance of this pressing social problem. In this chapter, governance is seen as a political setting in which to deal with shifts in issues and procedures, particularly with respect to issues of difference, values and conflicts over recognition and identity.[2] Governance thus describes a form of political decision-making and regulation that mirrors transition processes in that it includes not only governmental actors but also civil society actors. Governance processes attempt to integrate as many actors as possible with different views and preferences on the issues. Therefore, frames and

---

1   Funk, Nanette / Mueller, Magda (eds): Gender politics and post-communism. Reflections from Eastern Europe and the former Soviet Union, New York/NY: Routledge, 1993; Watson, Peggy: Eastern Europe's silent revolution. Gender, Sociology 1993 (Vol. 27), No. 3, pp. 471–488; Gal, Susan / Kligman, Gail: The Politics of Gender after Socialism, Princeton/NJ: Princeton University Press, 2000.

2   Hajer, Maarten A. / Wagenaar, Hendrik (eds): Deliberative Policy Analysis: Understanding Governance in the Network Society, Cambridge: Cambridge University Press, 2003.

social meanings deserve greater importance in the entire policy cycle and not just in governmental decision-making.[3]

Against this background, we seek to describe the governance process regarding domestic violence in four countries in CSEE, namely Slovenia, Croatia, Bosnia-Herzegovina and Bulgaria. In doing so, we look at the policy cycle, focusing primarily on agenda-setting and policy formation/formulation (e.g. institutional arrangements). Utilizing the concept of governance outlined above, we are especially interested in the processes of political participation and the interaction of state authorities and civil society protagonists. In addition, we will visit the question of how external factors/actors (e.g. the EU, foreign donors) have affected the governing of domestic violence.

5.2. The Governance Process

5.2.1. Agenda-Setting

Having been trigged by different factors, the recognition of domestic violence as a social problem started at different points of time in the four selected countries. Even under socialism Slovenia and Croatia had an active feminist scene, going back to the first Yugoslav feminist meetings in the 1970s. In 1987 Yugoslav feminists met in Ljubljana, where the fight against domestic violence was given centre stage. Following the meeting in Ljubljana, the Zagreb-based Women's Group Trešnjevka founded the first helpline in 1988 and in 1990 the first women's refuge in Eastern Europe. Shortly thereafter, in 1989, inspired by the Croatian experience, an association called 'SOS Telephone' (Društvo SOS telefon) was established as the first NGO working with women survivors of violence in Slovenia. The initial liberalization of the Communist system facilitated further collaboration among Yugoslav feminists, who started to organize discussions about legislative changes, women's political participation, etc. Before the final disintegration of Yugoslavia, feminist activists were planning to organize a meeting of the SOS Hotlines, the first three feminist services for women survivors of violence, to discuss the issue of domestic violence with activists from Ljubljana, Zagreb and Belgrade.[4] However, the collapse of Yugoslavia and the wars that followed brutally disrupted these early endeavours. While Slovenia was only marginally affected by the so-called Ten-Day War, Croatia was pulled into a heavy conflict from 1991 to 1995. As a result, the war imposed its own nationalistic agenda, totally disrupting the nascent debate on

---

3   Fischer, Frank: Reframing Public Policy. Discursive Politics and Deliberative Practices, Oxford: Oxford University Press, 2003.
4   Due to the unrestricted freedom of movement, Yugoslav feminists maintained contacts to European and international feminist organizations, allowing for communication and exchange of ideas, enriching and inspiring the Yugoslav debate, not least in the field of domestic violence.

domestic violence. A new discourse emerged, focusing on women victims of wartime rape, a topic intensively exploited in the propagandist media of all warring parties. According to Nela Pamukovic from the Autonomous Women's House Zagreb, nobody was interested in domestic violence during the war.[5] Moreover, there was strong pressure, including on women's organizations, to foster patriotism and national identity. It was only in the second half of the 1990s that Croat women's organizations were able to pick up the thread of their earlier activities. This process gained momentum in the post-Tudjman period under the Social Democratic Party (SDP)-led government, leading both to a reframing of the issue (from wartime rapes to domestic violence) and to significant legislative changes in this regard from 1999/2000 on.

Unlike Croatia, Slovenia's feminist activists were spared from war-related disruptions. By the early 1990s, new NGOs were established that worked with women survivors of violence (e.g. Association for Non-Violent Communication). The first non-governmental women's shelter in Slovenia was established in 1997. Slovenia had already joined the global campaign '16 Days of Activism against Gender Violence' in 1994 (Croatia in 1997). Additionally, in every year since 1999, a national media campaign entitled 'What's up, girl?' (Kaj ti je, deklica?) has been organized by the state-run Office for Equal Opportunities in collaboration with various NGOs (SOS telefon, Fiks, DNK, ŠOU, etc.). In contrast to Croatia, the Slovenian state had already proved itself to be fairly responsive to NGO demands in the early 1990s. The state established the first women's refuge in 1996 (CSD Maribor) even before the foundation of the first NGO-run shelter. Moreover, all thirteen existing shelters/safe houses in Slovenia have been subsidized by the state.

In Bosnia-Herzegovina, there was no feminist engagement on domestic violence in the 1980s. The reason was that an independent women's movement, let alone feminist activism like in Ljubljana, Zagreb and Belgrade, simply did not exist. As opposed to Croatia and Slovenia, addressing domestic violence was not spurred by feminist ideas and feminist activism, but sprang from the dreadful horror of mass wartime rapes. Duška Andrić-Ružičić from Medica Zenica explained that Bosnian feminism was born of necessity, and did not 'organically grow', as it had in Croatia and Slovenia, where a 'necessity' (i.e. the struggle against domestic violence) was recognized on the basis of pre-existing feminist convictions.[6] Due to the war-related isolation of the country, relevant international developments and debates on domestic violence passed largely unnoticed in Bosnia-Herzegovina in the first half of the 1990s. However, the Dayton Peace Accords, which brokered peace to Bosnia in 1995, resulted in a massive inflow of foreign aid and the large-scale engagement of the International Community in Bosnia, facilitating the development of civil society organizations, especially women's NGOs.

---

5   Interview with Nela Pamukovic, recorded in October 2007.
6   Interview with Duška Andrić-Ružičić, recorded in January 2008.

These internationally sponsored organizations have served as the backbone of the emerging women's movement in Bosnia-Herzegovina.

As one of the most rigid Warsaw Pact states, Bulgaria did not have any independent social organizations that might have tackled the issue of domestic violence under Communism. Besides that, the long-standing conviction that Communism had done more than enough for the equalization of women and men in Bulgaria meant that gender issues, including domestic violence, were largely disregarded. Thus, it was not until 1994 that some Bulgarian NGOs and primarily the Bulgarian Gender Research Foundation (BGRF) started to address the problem of domestic violence, in collaboration with the US-American NGO Minnesota Advocates for Human Rights.[7] Yet the primary inspiration for Bulgarian women's activists came from the Fourth World Conference on Women in Beijing (1995), which connected Bulgarian NGOs with similar organizations worldwide and revitalized the connection to the Minnesota Advocates. At the same time, with the assistance of international donors, the first local NGOs to provide support to women survivors of violence emerged (e.g. the Animus Association since 1994, and the Nadja Centre since 1995). However, according to Genoveva Tisheva from BGRF, the early discussion was dominated by the externally driven attention to trafficking in human beings and violence against children.[8] It was only later that this discussion was gradually expanded to include domestic violence and violence against women. Unlike Slovenia – and later Croatia – Bulgarian authorities ignored the issue of domestic violence for a long time, especially concerning financial support and infrastructure. There are only two shelters in Bulgaria (both NGO-run) at the moment (in a country with a population of approximately eight million people).[9] The state has been virtually absent from the financing of the shelters. The only exception has been the shelter in Silistra, where the municipality, led by a female mayor, decided to provide some funds from the municipal budget for 2005.[10]

As the previous discussion has made clear, the definition of domestic violence as a social problem, along with the process of actually setting it on the agenda, has

---

7   Minnesota was one of the first states in the USA to introduce a Protection against Domestic Violence Act in 1979. The Minnesota Advocates have been active in the region since the early 1990s. They played a decisive role later in the process of drafting the Bulgarian domestic violence bill, offering their twenty-five years of experience.

8   Interview with Genoveva Tisheva, recorded in February 2008.

9   The first shelter in the country was established by Center Nadja in Sofia in 1997. However, it was closed in 2003 due to a lack of funds after international donors had begun to withdraw their financial support. Cf.: Nadja Center Foundation, http://www.centrenadja.hit.bg/koismenie-eng. htm, accessed 15 May 2008.

10   This is the first and thus far only case where a local authority officially acknowledged the necessity of this social service. The shelter in Silistra was financed by international donors and the Agency for Social Support to the Ministry of Labour and Social Policy for the period 2000 to 2005. From January 2006 on it was partly financed by the state through the Ministry of Finance. Cf.: Open Society Institute: Violence against Women. Does the Government Care in Bulgaria?, Budapest: Open Society Institute, 2007, p. 41.

followed different patterns in the four selected countries. The common denomina-tor of all four case studies is the crucial role of the non-governmental sector. In none of the cases did the state initiate the agenda-setting process. Therefore, it was solely due to NGOs and individual activists that the significance of the issue was recognized and that a public debate on domestic violence was launched. However, the patterns and trigger factors were somewhat different. The agenda-setting process started in Slovenia and Croatia back in the Communist period, drawing on an indigenous fem-inist movement. Not least because of this early agenda-setting, public awareness of domestic violence as a social problem and the responsiveness of the state in Slovenia and Croatia have been the farthest advanced among the selected countries. Even in the case of war-related disruptions and a semi-authoritarian regime, as was the case in Croatia until 1999, the existence of an indigenous feminist scene appears to be a strong predictor for efficient agenda-setting.

Bulgaria and Bosnia-Herzegovina, countries with no indigenous feminist move-ments and no previous experience in dealing with domestic violence under Communist rule, tackled the issue much later on (not until the mid-1990s). In both cases external factors played a comparatively significant role. In Bosnia, the International Community nurtured and fostered the local civil society sector, in particular women's organiza-tions that initially worked with women survivors of wartime rape and later focussed on domestic violence. In contrast to Croatia, the war in Bosnia provided the initial spark for the engagement on domestic violence.

In Bulgaria it was the experience of the Beijing conference and the ample support of the Minnesota Advocates and many other international organizations that facilitated NGO engagement on domestic violence.[11] Accordingly, both Bulgarian and Bosnian women's NGOs have been highly dependent on external support. For this reason, the agenda-setting process in these two countries was fairly contingent upon the con-ceptions and priorities of external actors. Since state authorities were largely uninter-ested, even dismissive for a long time, (externally inspired and sponsored) NGOs came into being to fill the vacuum.

5.2.2. Policy Formation/Formulation

The agenda-setting processes have led to steady pressure on state administrations to take action and thus responsibility. Consequently, the authorities in all four countries have shown responsiveness to NGO demands, though to varying degrees. Despite some measures (e.g. Slovenian authorities established the first shelter in 1996), it was not until 1998/99 that any governmental policies on domestic violence emerged, albeit

11   Bulgarian NGOs such as Nadja Center and Animus in Sofia, Diva in Plovdiv and Demetra in Burgas were surely the result of local initiatives, yet not a single one of these organizations would have been able to survive without external (foreign) support.

largely on the legislative level. The first tentative legislative changes in the region took place within the scope of general laws, mostly via the criminalization of domestic violence in the Criminal Code.[12] However, these penal provisions were solely aimed at the perpetrators of violence, leaving aside the protection and empowerment of the survivors of violence. In order to remedy this, Slovenia and Croatia subsequently made further amendments, introducing e.g. bans on approaching a specific place or person[13] and restraining orders.[14] Although some of these measures appeared to work rather well,[15] the majority of NGOs argued that only a special law could provide effective protection from domestic violence. As in the agenda-setting phase, NGOs played an important role in the legislative process as well.

Slovenia was rather late to adopt the Family Violence Prevention Act (FVPA)[16], which came into effect in February 2008.[17] In accordance with the generally strong engagement of public institutions in the realm of gender equality,[18] the passage of the FVPA was a result of joint efforts by NGOs and governmental institutions. Although the NGOs had agitated for such a law since the mid-late 1990s, it was a special report on violence in the family by the Human Rights Ombudsman (2003/2004) that got the ball rolling. This document illuminated the problem of domestic violence, and recognized it as a widespread social problem requiring a solution at the national level. Following the assessment of the report, the then liberal government prepared the first draft of the FVPA, which was not introduced in Slovenian parliament due to the change of government. The new conservative administration put the bill on hold, mostly because the new Minister for Labour, Family and Social Affairs (MLFS), Janez Drobnic, strongly

---

12   All four countries had criminalized spousal rape by the 1990s, followed by the criminalization of domestic (or more precisely: family) violence. Domestic violence has been criminalized in Slovenia since 1999 (Article 299), in Croatia since 2000 (Art. 215a), and in Bosnia-Herzegovina since 2000 (Republika Srpska, Article 208) resp. 2003 (Federation BiH, Article 222). Bulgaria is the only country among the four that has not criminalized domestic violence in the Penal Code yet.

13   Cf.: Slovenian Criminal Procedure Act (1998/99) and Croatian Criminal Procedure Act (2002).

14   Cf.: Slovenian Police Act (2003).

15   Since their introduction into the Police Act in 2003, these measures have helped Slovenian police to issue an increasing number of restraining orders: 2005 – 154, 2006 – 277, 2007 – 488.

16   Zakon o preprečevanju nasilja v družini (ZPND), Uradni list RS, št. 16-487/2008, p. 1148.

17   However, even before the adoption of the FVPA, Slovenia established a rather sophisticated infrastructure to tackle the problem of domestic violence. Besides the legislative changes and state funds for thirteen women's shelters as mentioned above, twelve Regional Coordinators for the Problem of Violence in the Family were created in 2004. In addition, there has been an Expert Council for the problem of violence in the family within the Ministry for Labour, Family and Social Affairs since 2001. The gender equality bodies (e.g. Office for Equal Opportunities, formerly Women's Policy Office) have focused on domestic violence as well.

18   Slovenia was the first country in the region to establish a public body devoted to gender equality issues, namely the Women's Policy Office (since 1992), which also dealt with domestic violence. This development is attributed to the strong and powerful feminist movement in Slovenia. Jalušič, Vlasta / Antić, Milica G.: Women – Politics – Equal Opportunities. Prospects for Gender Equality in Central and Eastern Europe, Ljubljana: Peace Institute, 2001, p. 21.

opposed it. The legislative process was resumed only after he had been forced to resign (in December 2006). In July 2007 the MLFS presented a new draft to the public, offering NGOs the opportunity to comment and lobby for changes. In general, the FVPA has been described as systematic and comprehensive. However, further assessment is premature at this point because the implementation of the law has just started.

With its Law on Protection from Violence in the Family in 2003[19], Croatia was one of the first countries in the region to pass legislation of this kind. The legislative process was initiated by women's and human rights organizations during the term of office of the SDP-led government. The Autonomous Women's House Zagreb (AWHZ), B.a.B.e., and Centre for Women War Victims have been exceedingly involved in long-standing lobbying and public campaigns for the adoption of such a law.[20] AWHZ in particular has led the way since the mid-1980s, participating in the process of amending the Family Law (1998) and Criminal Code (1998, 2000, 2003) and helping to create the Law on Protection from Violence in the Family (2003).[21] The latter would have not been possible without the activists of AWHZ and B.a.B.e. who prepared the first draft of the law and submitted it in July 2002 to the Ministry of Justice, Penal Code Administration, and Criminal Regulations Department. However, even the strongest NGOs need allies in the government to initiate legislative changes. Not only the Social Democrat-led government (2000 – 2003), but also the conservative HDZ-led government (2003 –) proved to be fairly receptive to the NGOs' work. Jadranka Kosor (HDZ), the Deputy Prime Minister and Minister of Family, Veterans' Affairs and Intergenerational Solidarity, has been especially supportive of efforts to combat domestic violence.[22] In 2002, almost simultaneously to the creation of the NGO-run working group aimed at drafting the law, an official governmental task force was entrusted with the elaboration of the corresponding bill. Interestingly, one of the AWHZ lawyers, Ljubica Matijević-Vrsaljko, was appointed the head of this task force. Notwithstanding, AWHZ and Matijević-Vrsaljko failed to rally support for certain important points, and they particularly objected to the provision in the draft stipulating that domestic violence should be treated as a misdemeanour

---

19 Cf.: Zakon o zaštiti od nasilja u obitelji, Narodne novine, broj 116/03.
20 The criminalization of family violence in the Criminal Code can also be attributed to persistent lobbying of these (and some other) NGOs.
21 AWHZ's activists also actively participated in the task force for the creation of National Strategy against Domestic Violence and accompanying Protocol of Action in Domestic Violence Cases. Besides Neva Tölle from AWHZ, several other activists participated in the task force, namely Sadika Zvirkić, from Korak, Marijana Zrinka Jegrišek from SOS hotline/Women Help Now and Sanja Sarnavka from B.a.B.e. Cf.: Benčić, Sandra / Bego, Adriana: National Study on Domestic Violence against Women in Croatia, Zagreb, 2007, p. 139, http://www.ekviva.net/index.php?page=news&id=849, accessed May 2008.
22 Besides Jadranka Kosor and her State Secretary Zdenka Ninic, there are also other female politicians (MPs) who have made a stand for the fight against domestic violence. To mention just some of them: Durdja Adlesic (HSLS), Zeljka Antunovic (SDP), Snjezana Biga-Friganovic (SPD), etc.

rather than a criminal offence.[23] For this reason, AWHZ, B.a.B.e. and other NGOs started lobbying for amendments to the law immediately after its passage.[24]

In contrast to Slovenia and Croatia, Bulgaria and Bosnia-Herzegovina had not introduced any protective measures for victims of domestic violence before the enactment of special laws dealing with this issue.

Unlike the other three countries, Bulgaria failed to address domestic violence in its Criminal Code, which made the need for a special law even more urgent. The path to success was long and arduous, however. The driving force behind the law in Bulgaria was Genoveva Tisheva and her colleagues at BGRF. Long before the legislative process began, Tisheva and Minnesota Advocates had worked in partnership to push for legal reform on domestic violence.[25] Beginning with the Conference on Legal Strategies to Confront Domestic Violence in 1997, Minnesota Advocates consulted with BGRF in drafting the new civil order for protection law. As Cheryl Thomas so aptly puts it:

> Minnesota's history and experience with the creation and enforcement of civil order for protection laws was a source of information and guidance to the Bulgarian advocates as they worked on their own landmark law. BGRF and Minnesota Advocates exchanged many drafts of the proposed law over many months.[26]

In 2000 the draft law was at a point where it could be presented to the Ministry of Justice with the assistance of the American Bar Association. However, the Ministry refused the proposal. There was no political support for such a law at that time.

Based on this experience, BGRF decided to generate more publicity for the domestic violence bill by inviting Minnesota Advocates to present their experience with a similar law to parliamentarians, journalists, judges, government representatives, etc.[27] In the course of this campaign Bulgarian parliamentarian Marina Dikova took notice of BGRF's initiative and offered her assistance in the legislative process. She established an ad-hoc working group consisting of three parliamentarians and three NGO representatives. They proposed a slimmed-down version of the original draft[28] in order

---

23   Benčić, Sandra / Bego, Adriana: National Study on Domestic Violence against Women in Croatia, Zagreb, 2007, p. 139, http://www.ekviva.net/index.php?page=news&id=849, accessed May 2008.

24   During this process AWHZ distributed policy recommendations to various institutions. Neva Tölle, director of the AWHZ, was regularly invited to sessions of relevant parliamentary committees. During the last amendments to the Law on Protection from Violence in the Family, Sanja Bencic from B.a.B.e was the only NGO representative in the working group that elaborated the amendments to the law. Cf.: Benčić, Sandra / Bego, Adriana: National Study on Domestic Violence against Women in Croatia, Zagreb, 2007, p. 139.

25   Thomas, Cheryl: The Power and Pain of Partnerships. The Minnesota Bulgaria Connection, Center on Women and Public Policy Case Study Program, Humphrey Institute of Public Affairs, University of Minnesota, 2005, p. 3.

26   Ibid., p. 4.

27   Ibid., p. 1.

28   Several provisions were removed: funding for victim services, criminalization of violation of protection order, criminalization of violence in homosexual relationships, etc.

to enhance its chances for adoption. Dikova lobbied hard in her party for the law.[29] Genoveva Tisheva describes this effort as follows:

> This was a difficult process. Even the people in Marina's party and in the parliament were not convinced [by] the new instrument. Everybody was against the violence in families, but nobody wanted to take harsh measures – infringement on human rights![30]

Dikova's initial attempt to get the bill through the relevant parliamentary committee failed. But then she managed to win over the Minister of Justice. Within two weeks the Minister convened a task force to finalize the existing bill. The bill was introduced in the Parliament in June 2003 and adopted rather laggingly in March 2005.[31]

Bosnia-Herzegovina did not have a strong feminist movement to draw on before the war. However, the massive inflow of foreign aid after the war created quite a vivid NGO landscape in Bosnia, with women's organizations particularly preferred by international donors. These newly created NGOs were the driving force behind the initiative to adopt a law on domestic violence in Bosnia. After the criminalization of family violence in the Criminal Codes of Republika Srpska (2000) and the Federation of Bosnia-Herzegovina (2003), Bosnia adopted a far-reaching law on gender equality that addressed gender-based violence (!) as well, including (sexual) harassment, which was the first reference to EU anti-discrimination policy in a Bosnian law. The Gender Equality Act contains a comprehensive catalogue of sanctions for the offence of gender-based violence, including imprisonment of up to five years. This law was jointly drafted by NGOs, IGOs[32], bilateral donors (Finland), local gender equality bodies and state institutions. However, the Gender Equality Act did not stipulate any protective measures for survivors of gender-based violence, which induced women's NGOs to continue to demand a civil order for protection law.

A countrywide NGO network, the so-called Safe Network, which consists of thirty-three NGOs working in the field of domestic violence, started the initiative for the adoption of a Law on Protection from Violence in the Family.[33] The inspiration for the law emanated from concrete problems in their work with women survivors of domestic violence. There were a lot of cases that could not be solved within the existing legal framework. At that time, the executive director of the government Gender Centre of the Federation BiH (GC FBiH) was Samra Filipovic-Hadziabdic, who was sympathetic towards the cause and helped the law to gain momentum. In other words, NGOs ini-

---

29 Marina Dikova was member of the then ruling party, National Movement Simeon II, founded in 2001 by Simeon II Sachsen-Coburg-Gotha.
30 Interview with Genoveva Tisheva, recorded in February 2008.
31 At the moment, we do not have a satisfying explanation for this long period of time between the introduction of the bill and its adoption.
32 The most important International Governmental Organization (IGO) in this process was the UN Office of the High Commissioner for Human Rights (OHCHR).
33 Basically, the moving power behind this initiative was the twelve strongest NGOs in the Network, organized in the so-called Counselling Body.

tiated the law, and the GC FBiH organized the law-making process, since the NGOs were not strong enough to do so. The GC FBiH invited some NGOs to contribute to the process by participating in working groups, providing content, etc. Unlike other initiatives, where the International Community played a decisive role, the adoption of the Protection against Family Violence Act was a local initiative, inspired and launched by home-grown NGOs.

The legislative process in the other Bosnian entity,[34] Republika Srpska (RS), began first as a joint process with the Federation of Bosnia-Herzegovina (FBiH) with the objective of adopting one law for the whole country. However, after a while it was decided to enact two separate laws. The NGOs in RS[35] had been lobbying for such a law ever since the criminalization of family violence in 2000. However, even after the state institutions (Gender Centre of RS, Ministry of Justice) embraced the initiative, only one NGO representative was allowed to participate in the consultations. RS authorities generally showed little interest in welcoming the NGOs' proposals. Given this reluctant stance, the support of two dedicated female politicians was crucial for the success of the whole process. Nada Tesanovic, the Deputy President of the RS Assembly, and Ivka Ristic, the president of the Parliamentary Committee for Gender Equality in the RS Assembly, both members of the ruling party in RS, maintained good contacts to women's NGOs, providing them with access to important documents and information on parliamentary procedure.[36]

5.3. Concluding Remarks

In all four countries the driving forces behind the governance of domestic violence were civil society organizations, or, more precisely, women's organizations. Our short analysis of the governance process has revealed some general, cross-national patterns:

First and foremost, the influence of women's NGOs was significant in all phases of the governance process, being the strongest in the agenda-setting phase and somewhat weaker in the policy formulation/institutionalization phase, primarily due to the increasing engagement of state institutions. Non-state actors were able to mobilize significant resources and induce the state to take action in the field of domestic violence prevention.

---

34 The Dayton Peace Agreement set down the constitutional framework establishing Bosnia and Herzegovina as a state consisting of two entities, namely the Serb-dominated Republika Srpska (RS) and the Federation of Bosnia and Herzegovina (FBiH), mainly populated by Croats and Bosnian Muslims (Bosniaks).

35 Above all the United Women and Helsinki Citizens' Assembly from Banja Luka.

36 This political support is also crucial for the further development of the legal framework in Republika Srpska. For instance, the Law on Protection from Family Violence is currently being amended. The chance that the amendments proposed by the NGOs will pass is rather high, primarily due to the support of Nada Tesanovic and Ivka Ristic.

In all four cases, there was a political 'window of opportunity' that was conducive to the adoption of laws on domestic violence. In Slovenia, the legislative process could only be resumed after the dismissal of the conservative Minister for Labour, Family and Social Affairs, Janez Drobnic. The semi-authoritarian government of Croatia's Franjo Tudjman prevented any serious engagement on domestic violence. It was not until the change of government in 2000 that the state showed more responsiveness to NGO demands. In the Bosnian entity Republika Srpska, the new SNSD-led government boosted two women politicians onto the political scene who openly supported NGO endeavours for passing a special law on protection from family violence. In 2001, an unprecedented number of women were elected to the Bulgarian parliament.[37] One of them, Marina Dikova, strongly supported the cause of Bulgarian women's NGOs, and lobbied hard for the adoption of the Act on Domestic Violence.

Consequently, even the strongest NGOs would not have been able to reach the institutionalization phase of the governance process without responsive state authorities or at least allies in the political system. Political allies proved to be especially decisive in shifting from the agenda-setting to the institutionalization phase. Female politicians/parliamentarians provided access to the political system for NGOs, which was crucial for the initiation and in the end also for the success of the legislative process.

NGOs managed to motivate the state to enact certain laws, but they did not succeed in achieving some of their more substantive goals. The most obvious failure is the name of the special laws in the region: not a single one contains any reference to women or gender. In the best-case scenario, the law contains 'domestic violence' in the title (as in Bulgaria), but as a rule, 'violence in the family' is as close as it gets. This speaks volumes about the underlying intentions of the legislature. There has never been sufficient political support for laws tackling exclusively gender-based violence or violence against women. In some cases, the authorities even decided to characterize acts of domestic violence solely as a misdemeanour act rather than as a criminal offence (Croatia and Republika Srpska), which sends a clear signal with respect to the significance ascribed to domestic violence.

Because the EU introduced anti-discrimination standards to the new or acceding member states, we originally assumed that the EU accession process could have been relevant for the governance of domestic violence. Yet the EU's effect turned out to be very limited. The adoption and especially the implementation of anti-discrimination legislation, let alone in the area of domestic violence, had been neither carefully monitored nor an issue of priority at any stage during the accession talks. Even in the countries that were already members of the EU (Slovenia and Bulgaria) at the

---

37   The 39th National Assembly had the highest share of women ever: approx. 27%. Furthermore, 36.5% of the NDSV's seats in parliament were given to women. The National Movement Simeon the Second (NDSV), founded by former King Simeon of Bulgaria, won the majority of votes in the 2001 elections (43%).

time, the direct influence of the EU on the governance of domestic violence appears to have been next to none. However, some indirect influences surely exist. First, the EU has facilitated general openness of the political system towards non-state actors, enabling direct and indirect participation of women's NGOs in the legislative process.

Second, the EU has served as a 'metaphor' that was often employed by NGOs in order to convince state authorities to accept this or that international standard. And third, the EU has financed women's organizations and their work. Just to mention one case: the EU provided initial funds for the establishment of the first women's refuge in Republika Srpska. Especially in Bosnia-Herzegovina and Bulgaria, the impact of external actors can hardly be overstated. Without foreign support there would hardly be any of these engaged women's organizations actually making a difference.

And last but not least: the existence of an indigenous feminist movement appears to be a strong predictor for success throughout the governance process. Besides that, strong feminist activism is also crucial for the sustainability of legislative efforts. Only laws that are actually applied really matter. NGO-run monitoring of law implementation is therefore essential for the overall impact of the law. And in the end, that is what matters most.

Part II. Changing Perceptions, Values and
Identities

Raluca Prelipceanu

6. Highly-Skilled Migration and Societal Transformation in Romania. Implications for EU Integration

6.1. A Picture of the Romanian Highly-Skilled Migration during and after Communism

The collapse of communism brought about sweeping changes in the migratory patterns of Eastern Europeans. The beginning of the 1990s saw an upsurge of forms of mobility in Eastern Europe. Some of these were new, while others were merely the amplification of forms already present in the Eastern migratory space during communism. Many studies on Romanian migration emphasize the mobility of low-skilled workers, who often migrated illegally (and made the headlines of European newspapers); the mobility of the highly skilled tends to be ignored. In reality, highly-skilled migration flows developed in parallel with low-skilled flows.

Even if the mobility of the highly skilled has seen an important upsurge in recent years, Romania faced a brain drain on a smaller scale even during the communist period. As part of the ethnic migration agreements concluded with Israel, Hungary and Germany and also of an agreement with the US, almost 300,000 persons left Romania during the 1980s. The majority of these persons had a tertiary education level acquired in Romania. Besides these countries, the Romanian Ministry of Home Affairs also acknowledged flows of qualified Romanians to France, Canada and Australia. Thus, brain drain is not a new form of mobility but one which has experienced important transformations and developments since the fall of communism.

Romania ranked among the top thirty countries in terms of its stock of highly-skilled migrants in 2000, with a total of 176,393 Romanian nationals living abroad.[1] About 54.3% of these highly-skilled migrants lived in North America, with only 29.3% residing in EU countries and another 12.3% in other European countries. But even considering the preference of the migrants for North America, Romania still ranked among the top twenty-five countries supplying highly-skilled migrants to the EU-15.[2]

As the development of this form of mobility has become particularly clear in recent years, the study of the flows allows for an analysis which is even more interesting. In 2005, more than a quarter of Romanian emigrants were highly skilled, the rate being

---

1 Docquier, Frédéric / Marfouk, Abdeslan: International migration by educational attainment (1990–2000). Release 1.1, Policy Report DP, Washington D. C.: World Bank, 2005.

2 Docquier, Frédéric / Lohest, Olivier / Marfouk, Abdeslan: Union européenne et migrations internationales. L'UE15 contribue-t-elle à l'exode des travailleurs qualifiés?, in: Revue Economique, 2005 (Vol. 56), No. 6, pp. 1301–1330.

slightly higher in the case of men (28.5%) than of women (25.1%), as reported by the National Institute of Statistics (2005). Whereas the US and Canada are the main destinations for highly-skilled Romanians, Romania along with Turkey also ranks first as a country of origin for highly-skilled foreign residents in the enlarged Europe (which includes also ex-USSR and ex-Yugoslav countries and Turkey)[3].

At the EU-15 level in the early 1990s, most highly-skilled Romanians went to Germany,[4] but this no longer held true in 2000. What we have seen is a diversification of the destinations of highly-skilled Romanians in the EU-15. Radu has shown that the countries with the highest selectivity rate for Romanian migrants among the EU-15 are France and the United Kingdom, whereas Germany came third with a rate of selectivity just slightly exceeding the EU-15 average.[5]

The persons involved in this type of mobility are mostly young. A study conducted by the Open Society Foundation showed that more than 15,000 young people have been leaving Romania every year for the last six years once they finished their studies and a quarter of high-school students intended to leave during their undergraduate studies or after. According to the Romanian Passport Department and the Frontier Police, the rate of return for those who leave to study abroad is a mere 10%.

6.2. The Romanian Community in France

According to OECD estimates, there are about 10,000 highly-skilled Romanians in France, which represents a quarter of the Romanians living in France; another 10,000 were in an illegal situation before Romania joined the EU. However, the precise number of Romanians in France remains a mystery. The Romanian authorities place it at around 60,000, while informal sources often speak of 100,000. According to these sources, about 40,000 live in Paris and Ile-de-France, whereas the rest are spread all over the French territory. The most important poles of Romanian communities can be found near Strasbourg, Lille, Lyon (which has an important Roma community), Marseille, Montpellier and Bordeaux.[6]

France is one of the traditional destinations for Romanian migrants. Throughout Romania's history, France has represented a model for Romania and the ties established with this country have been particularly strong. We can identify several waves of Romanian highly-skilled migration to France. First of all, a wave of Romanian intellectuals and aristocrats exiled themselves to France during the early days of the communist

3   OCDE: Perspectives des migrations internationals, Paris: OCDE, 2006.
4   Straubhaar, Thomas: International Mobility of the Highly Skilled. Brain Gain, Brain Drain or Brain Exchange, Working Paper No. 88, HWWA, 2000.
5   Radu, Dragos: Human Capital Content and Selectivity of Romanian Emigration. Luxembourg Income Study, Working Paper No. 365, 2003.
6   Michaud, Marion: La Communauté roumaine en France, Fonds Européen pour la Liberté de l'Expression, 1995.

regime in Romania between 1946 and 1948. Even at the end of the 1950s, some Romanian intellectuals managed to arrive in France either as tourists, or simply because the communist leadership thought it best to get rid of persons perceived as a threat to the new regime and granted them the right to join family already in France.

Another wave had its origin in the labour migration from Romania during the 1960s, when, under specific labour agreements, some Romanian specialists went to work in North African countries. Once their contracts had ended, some of these people, mostly scientists, never returned to Romania, but instead went to France and obtained political refugee status.

During the 1990s, with the dismantling of political frontiers, many intellectuals fled abroad, some of them choosing France. Following the invasion of Bucharest by miners in the summer of 1990, a sign of possible political instability to come, it is estimated that 5,000 Romanian students left the country. The departures continued throughout the 1990s, with many Romanians leaving during their undergraduate studies. As the status of political refugee became more and more difficult to acquire and labour contracts favoured very specific domains (such as high tech fields), this strategy was adopted by a wider range of highly-skilled persons coming from other fields in order to later gain access to the foreign labour market. With the emergence of a network of student exchange programmes, France rapidly became one of the main destinations for study abroad.[7] However, this proved to be a mere strategy for leaving the country, with many students never coming back. In fact, the rate of return was so small that France reconsidered its policies in this area, and tried to develop joint programmes that would encourage Romanian students to return home once their studies were finished.

In light of Romania's future accession to the EU, the further development of these programmes led to an important increase in the number of those who left the country in early 2000. Focusing on Romanians who have migrated to France within the last ten years, our study is mostly concerned with this fourth and last wave of Romanian migration. We must emphasize that the conditions under which this wave developed are very different from those concerning the former three. In this case, Romania's accession to the EU was clearly in view and political conditions could no longer be considered unstable. The rate of growth of the Romanian economy was steadily increasing and foreign enterprises were investing in highly-skilled intensive sectors of the Romanian economy, creating the opportunity for well-paid jobs. For the first two waves, which took place during communism, there was no possibility of return and all ties with the country of origin and with those left behind were severed for what seemed to be forever. The third wave developed under the difficult conditions of the Romanian transition, characterized by no economic opportunities and the worsening

---

7   Lagrave, Rose-Marie: *Voyage dans un pays de l'utopie déchoue*, Paris: PUF, 1998.

of living conditions. Compared to the former waves, for which the future seemed clearly defined and rooted in the country of destination, we can consider the future prospects of this last wave as being open ended.

6.3.   Case study. Romanian Highly-Skilled Migrants in France in the Last Ten Years

Our case study relies on twenty exploratory interviews that we conducted in France during March and April 2006. We then drew up a questionnaire that was filled in by 125 persons. Our sample can be described as follows. As previously mentioned, this most recent form of mobility concerns mostly youth and 48% of our sample fell between the ages of twenty-six and thirty. All these persons had a tertiary education acquired either in Romania or France. The average time already spent in France by these people ranged from two to five years. Two thirds of our sample population was made up of women, which is in accordance with studies by Badie and de Wenden.[8]

As the history of migrants begins in their country of origin, we will first investigate who these people were before their departure from Romania. First of all, they were among the best and brightest Romanian students. They came from all eight NUTS II level regions and from thirty-three out of the forty-one Romanian counties. As a region of origin, the capital Bucharest-Ilfov ranked first with 27.2% of the migrants. Another 16.8% came from the North-Eastern region and 14.4% from the South-Muntenia region. As far as universities are concerned, the primacy of the universities of Bucharest is clear, with 54.4% of the sample having studied there. Bucharest is followed by the universities of Cluj and Iasi.

We can thus identify a 'capital' effect, with Bucharest attracting an important number of Romanian students due to the quality and the diversity of the studies offered there as well as to the availability of better job opportunities upon graduation.

In terms of the fields of specialization, among men we identify mostly high tech specialists (32.6%) and economists (30.4%), followed by mathematicians, while among women we identify mostly economists (34.2%) and philologists (15.2%). The diversity of fields is greater in the case of women. Six of the individuals in our sample had a double degree and nine had completed their entire college education in France.

The main advantage that this population has obviously resides in the skills they have acquired. Most of them had had a previous migratory experience generally linked to their studies. If internal migration (which sixty-two persons in our sample had undertaken) or international migration (eight persons), or even both types (four persons) are taken into consideration, we can identify the existence of a mobility experience that

---

8   Badie, Bertrand / Wihtol de Wenden, Catherine: Le défi migratoire. Questions de relations inter-
        nationales, Paris: Presses de Sciences Politiques, 1994.

would play an important role in these individuals' subsequent decision to emigrate and in the way they fared afterwards. There are even cases in which an entire family partook in the 'culture of mobility', with several members living in other countries or having spent significant time abroad.

Although these people generally arrived in France as international students, this was often a stepping stone to their entry into the labour market of the destination country. Meyer and Hernandez[9] have observed that two thirds of R&D experts on the global level entered the destination country as students. As Steven Vertovec underlines, 'the experience of being a foreign student significantly increases the likelihood of being a skilled migrant at a later stage.'[10] The networks developed by the students helped to provide opportunities for others from the country of origin.

6.4. Reasons for Departure and the Main Strategies Employed

The most important reason for departure seems to be the desire to pursue internationally recognized studies leading to the acquisition of an internationally recognized diploma. The second reason is the search for better job opportunities and the desire to acquire a better social status. These two reasons are not mutually exclusive, however; a diploma recognized all over the world seems to be the element facilitating the mobility. Once the diploma is acquired, graduates can go wherever they find the best job opportunities. Another element motivating departure is discontent with Romanian society; many feel that even though the communist regime is gone, the change in mentality has lagged behind. Some participants in our study said that they left in search of freedom, which they perceived as still difficult to find in the Romanian society. At the same time, the desire to experience another culture also plays a significant part. Humankind's exploratory nature persists even in modern times.

Amongst the strategies employed to leave Romania, study abroad plays, as expected, the most important part. France is the country that receives the greatest number of Romanian students each year. In 2004, 4,839 Romanian students attended courses in French universities. Almost 70% of our sample population left the country as international students, whereas a few individuals left with a work contract (mostly high tech professionals) or for the purpose of reuniting with family (in the case of women). Some of these strategies require a well-organized plan, for in order to become an international student, one needs to have very good marks and to work for them several years in advance.

9   Meyer, Jean-Baptiste / Hernandez, Valeria: Les diasporas scientifiques et techniques. État de lieu, in: Nedelcu, Mihaela (ed.): La mobilité internationale des compétences. Situations récentes, approches nouvelles, Paris: L'Harmattan, 2004.

10   Vertovec, Steven: Transnational Networks and Skilled Labour Migration, Ladenburger Diskurs 'Migration', Gottlieb Daimler- und Karl Benz-Stiftung, Ladenburg, 2002.

Sometimes, the strategies foresaw a change of status after immigration, for example from international students to highly-skilled workers or from tourists to international students. The boundaries between the categories are fairly fluid, as one can very easily pass from one to another.

6.5. Destination Choice and Performance in the Labour Market

What determines the choice of the destination country? In the majority of cases, the decision seems to be shaped by the exchange programmes offered by the universities in the countries of origin and destination. Formal networks are the main channels of mobility for the highly-skilled, as described by Faist.[11] French 'soft power'[12] also seems to play an important role, as knowledge of the French language and the allure of French culture together represent one of the most important elements spurring the choice to go to France. French soft power is very important in the Romanian case, as Romanian students began migrating to France at the end of the eighteenth century. This even became a tradition in the following century, when aristocratic families sent their children to be educated in France. Consequently, with respect to the history of French-Romanian relations, the exchange not only of people, but also of ideas, practices and symbols, should be emphasized. This flow was interrupted only by the communist period.

Another factor that seems to have influenced the choice of destination is the existence of informal networks of kin or friends. About a third of our sample cited the importance of informal networks in their choice of destination. The development of new information and communication technologies (ICTs) in recent years has facilitated contact within the networks, allowing for a virtual projection of the future space of mobility. Friends and kin already situated in the country of destination send information via virtual channels to future migrants in the home country. Moreover, migrants can do their own virtual search and gather information (including visual images) about their destinations. Migrants can in this way become accustomed to their future destination even before having physical contact with the place of destination. In other cases, due to the significant decrease in transportation costs, many migrants in our sample had already been to the destination country to visit relatives and friends. The visits paid as tourists were just a first step to becoming a migrant and were part of a learning process that was very important for the future mobility of the migrants.

---

11   Faist, Thomas: Transnationalization in international migration. Implications for the study of citizenship and culture, ESRC Transnational Communities Programme Working Paper WPTC-99-14, Oxford, 1999.
12   Nye, Joseph S.: Soft power. The means to success in world politics, Cambridge/MA: Perseus Books, 2004.

Focusing this time on the destination country, we would like to know why these students stayed on once their study period had ended. Some of the respondents admitted to have stayed on in order to complete their qualification, whereas the majority felt that they would have better career opportunities if they stayed in France.

In the case of researchers, the lack of possibilities to conduct research at the international level in Romania and the low rate of investment in R&D both in the public and the private sectors seemed to encourage them to stay on in France. Returning to the home country was perceived as leading to brain waste.

For others, their decision to stay on was mainly due to changes that took place in their lives. Some of them built families in France; others simply felt that they had created their own lives there and that going back to Romania would mean having to start all over again.

How do these migrants fare in their destination country? At the professional level, the difficulties emerge with the passage from one status to another, for instance from international student to highly-skilled worker. Many of those in our sample admitted to having difficulties in finding a job commensurate with their qualifications. Their success also depended on their chosen professions and thus on labour market demand. If the economists and the high tech specialists seemed to face relatively fewer difficulties in finding a job, this was not the case for people with humanities degrees. Most of the migrants blamed this state of affairs on discrimination against foreigners in the French labour market. Indeed, the unemployment rate stood in 2002 at 5% for the natives, 7.2% for EU-15 nationals on the French labour market, 11% for foreigners having acquired French nationality and at 18% for foreigners coming from countries other than the EU-15, a rate almost three and a half times greater than in the case of the native-born population.[13]

6.6. Multiple Allegiances and Identity

If professional integration can be difficult, what about social integration? Among the factors that can facilitate social integration are the acquisition of French citizenship (which ensures judicial rights equal to those enjoyed by the natives), knowledge of the French language, marriage to a French citizen, and kin and friendship networks, which can ease the immigrants' contact with the communities in which they find themselves. The most important part is played by the ties developed with colleagues at the university or at work; these people introduce the migrants to common practices and act as their best teachers.

Upon analysing the interviews we conducted, we realized that the traditional discourse in terms of social integration, assimilation and identity no longer corresponds

---

13   Economic and Social Council: L'Insertion des Jeunes d'Origine Etrangère, 2002.

to these migrants' experiences, because they live in a world of multiple allegiances. These allegiances are to the home society, the destination society and, above all, to a multitude of communities.[14]

We indeed notice that these migrants develop competing but not exclusive attachments to more than one community at the same time. We can identify a wide range of communities to which these migrants belong: family communities, professional communities, student communities, ethnic communities, religious communities and political communities. These migrants are thus part of a range of overlapping communities both in real and symbolic terms. They can actually belong to more than one type of community, and even to more than one community of the same type. As Rainer Bauböck notes, 'Multiple citizenships are the most visible illustration of overlapping membership in political communities.'[15]

In these communities migrants very often develop ties that go beyond borders, thus creating a network culture, as most of them report having friends or relatives in other EU countries. Van Hear identifies three types of factors favouring the development of cross-border ties: communication facilities, transportation development and socio-cultural competences.[16] According to Ascher,

> these new social ties are probably weaker, less polyvalent, but a lot more numerous and changing: they grant mobility a new social status and allow individuals to lead a life of n dimensions.[17]

These cross-border ties provide the migrants with access to information and events that occur in more than one place at the same time. The nature of these ties can be either virtual, in which case the contact inside the network occurs via the internet, or via mobile or fixed phones, or face to face. Virtual technology allows migrants to be present in several places at once. With the fall in transportation costs, migrants can easily circulate between the physical spaces that support the network. Identity itself is rebuilt inside these networks. Multiple allegiances to different communities are at the heart of the shift from a 'territorial identity to a network identity'[18]. In this context,

---

14   Kastoryano, Riva: Individus, communautés, états. Le cas des migrants de Turquie en Europe, in: Cahiers d'étude sur la Méditerranée Orientale et le monde turco-iranien, 1998, No. 26, pp. 105–123.

15   Bauböck, Rainer: Political community beyond the sovereign state. Supranational federalism and transnational minorities, in: Vertovec, Steven / Cohen, Robin (eds): Conceiving Cosmopolitanism. Theory, Context and Practice, Oxford: Oxford University Press, 2002, pp. 110–136, here p. 134.

16   Van Hear, Nicholas: New Diasporas. The Mass Exodus, Dispersal and Regrouping of Migrant Communities, Seattle: University of Washington Press, 1998.

17   Ascher, François: L'individu mobile dans une société hypermoderne, in: Kaplan, D. / Lafont, H. (eds): Mobilités.net, Paris: L.G.D.J, 2004, pp. 45–50, here p. 46.

18   Badie, Bertrand: La fin des territoires. Essai sur le désordre international et sur l'utilité sociale du respect, Paris: Fayard, 1995.

identity is also, inescapably, about displacement and relocation, the experience of sustaining and mediating complex affiliations, multiple attachments.[19]

As a consequence, identities tend to be more situational. They are overlapping and flexible in order to allow individuals to adapt to their new mobility and to take advantage of the best opportunities they come across.

6.7. Contacts and Emergence of a Network Culture

Network expansion usually precedes territorial expansion. Within the network, material and immaterial flows circulate, ensuring the transmission of goods and services, as well as of social and economic information. The information received about better career opportunities often spurs the departure of migrants to another country. Social networks usually guide migrants into or through specific places and occupations. They are often crucial for finding jobs and housing.[20] Multiple presences allow migrants to take advantage of better career opportunities no matter where these might turn up. Migrants do not circulate only between their home country and their destination country, but actually have multiple destinations. What determines their mobility is the search for a better social status and better career opportunities. Should these opportunities arise in the home country, these migrants might return; if not, they are likely to choose another destination. With Romania's accession to the EU, some indeed seem convinced that better opportunities might surface in Romania. But even if they return home, they will no longer be confined to a certain space: they can go mobile again whenever they choose.

This space of flows is the source of their power, as it provides them with access to knowledge and information that are only available to individuals who are part of the network. We can actually identify the emergence of a network culture built by these migrants. This culture does not exclude friends and relatives who are still sedentary, however; differences between the different categories tend to fade away, and immobile individuals exposed to this network culture can easily become mobile. Conversely, mobile individuals can also choose to remain sedentary for a while. In this case, some specific effects for the country of origin come from the networks established with the migrants' families and friends but also with other professionals left behind. It is on these immaterial effects that we have chosen to focus on in our study. These long-distance networks can provide very important channels for flows of capital, skill and information.

---

19   Clifford, James: Mixed feelings, in: Cosmopolitics. Thinking and Feeling Beyond the Nation, Minneapolis/MN: University of Minnesota Press, 1998, pp. 362–370, here p. 369

20   Vertovec, Steven: Transnational Networks and Skilled Labour Migration, Ladenburger Diskurs 'Migration', Gottlieb Daimler- und Karl Benz-Stiftung, Ladenburg, 2002.

In our study, we try to assess the level of contact with families and friends back in the home country. For almost 40% of the migrants, these contacts take place weekly. For almost 50%, these contacts are even more frequent, occurring daily or several times a week. The preferred means of communication is the telephone in about 45% of the cases and the internet in 32%. The rest of the migrants use both means at the same frequency. The telephone still remains the dominant means of communication despite the development of the internet. This growth has resulted in the transformation of these 'objects of connection', i.e. the internet and the telephone, so that they have come to include each other's functions. The mobile phone allows one to connect to the internet, and the internet has spawned a line of services, like Skype and Messenger, with voice transmitting functions similar to those of the telephone. There is no clear distinction anymore between these objects, and by using one of them, the customer can actually be using the other at the same time.

The decrease in the price of communications allows migrants to maintain contact and actively take part in the real lives of those left behind. It is a way of living together and apart at the same time. The webcam attached to the computer makes face-to-face contact possible even in the case of virtual communication, reinforcing the impression of actual presence. Migrants are no longer absent from their space of origin, and their presence is ensured by the constant contact facilitated by the development of these means of communication. The eye is the 'most direct and purest interaction that exists'[21]. It generates the most complete reciprocity in the entire sphere of human relationships' since 'one cannot take through the eye without at the same time giving'[22]. In this way, the eye intensifies the connection and interaction of individuals. At the same time, the increased accessibility and velocity of modern transportation facilitates 'real' contact, allowing migrants to come back to their home country several times a year and enabling their family and friends to visit them in the destination country.

The flows of social capital determined by the contact can be very important. Recent interviews conducted with the friends and families of the migrants brought us to acknowledge that these flows lead to a learning process for those left in the home country. The mere existence of contact is not enough to guarantee the success of transfers. The family and friends back home need to have an absorption capacity allowing them to correctly decrypt the messages received. In order to facilitate contact and to ensure the accurate decryption of messages, family members have to take up practices they were not accustomed to before. The Absence and the presence can no longer be thought of as being in opposition, as migrants can nowadays be absent and present at the same time. Their presence is ensured by the development of network ties and the existence of contact – either virtual or real.

---

21   Simmel, Georg: Simmel on Culture, London: Sage, 1997, p. 111.
22   Ibid., p. 112.

6.8. Conclusions

The form of highly-skilled mobility that involves a lot of circulation between more than two countries can no longer be classified as brain drain. During the communist period, the highly-skilled migration from Romania could indeed be termed as brain drain, but nowadays, the strong ties with the home country and the development of contacts with the home society positively affecting its evolution renders the term brain drain obsolete. The networks that are developed ensure the flow of financial capital, knowledge and information. The individuals involved in these networks form the basis of a network culture that relies on both material and immaterial flows.

Romanian citizens abroad might actually play a very important part in the process of European integration, as integration means not only economic convergence but also convergence to the value system promoted by European countries. Through the immaterial flows that take place inside the networks, Romanian migrants can act as important catalysts for the transformation of Romanian society and for the convergence of Romanian values and lifestyles towards European values and lifestyles. This kind of convergence could be vital for Romanian society: informal institutions have been acknowledged to have played a major role in post-communist transition. The convergence of informal institutions seems to be in this case even more important than economic convergence. The persistence of behaviours inherited from the communist regime, like generalized corruption and clientelist networks, have constituted major drawbacks to the successful transformation of Romania. Without informal institutions that could legitimize and sustain economic reforms, economic convergence is unlikely to be achieved easily. When migration networks act in favour of this informal institutional convergence via flows, we consider this transformation to be a sort of transformation from below (imposed by migrants and their family and friends) and not something that is imposed by the Romanian state.

Elitsa Dimitrova

7.   Family and Reproduction in Post-Socialist Bulgaria. Towards a New Demographic Transition

7.1.   Introduction

The period following the end of socialism in Bulgaria was characterized by substantial changes in individual marital and reproductive behaviour. The postponement of childbearing and the overall reduction of fertility have led to a profound transformation of the country's demographic profile.

Figure 7-1:   Total Fertility Rate (TFR) and Mean Age at Birth of First Child in Bulgaria, 1960–2006

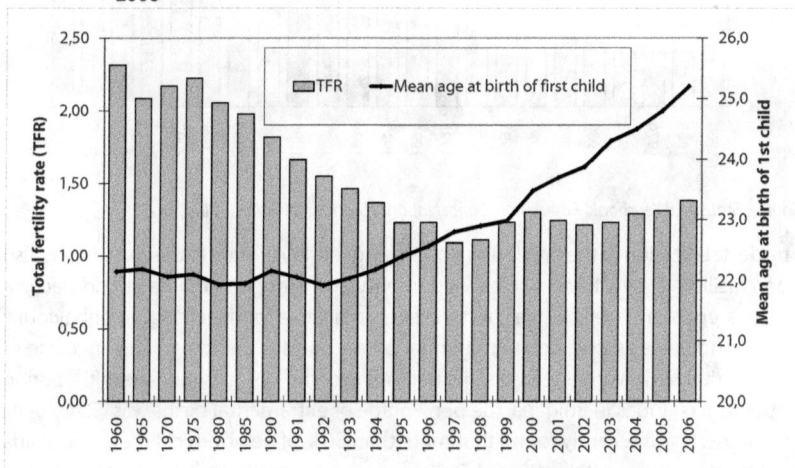

Source: Statistical Yearbook. Population, Sofia: National Statistical Institute, 2007, pp. 23–24.

The decrease of the total fertility rate to the 'lowest low fertility levels' in Europe (below 1.3 children per woman)[1] was followed by a significant tempo distortion caused by the changing age pattern of fertility. In particular, the mean age at birth of first child became 25.2 in 2006, whereas the indicator fluctuated around a value of 22 years in the beginning of the 1990s.[2] As a result, the recent demographic profile of the country

---

1   Kohler, Hans-Peter / Billari, Francesco C. / Ortega, José Antonio: The Emergence of Lowest-Low Fertility in Europe during the 1990s, in: Population and Development Review, 2002 (Vol. 28), No. 4, pp. 641–680, here p. 642.
2   Statistical Yearbook. Population, Sofia: National Statistical Institute, 2007, pp. 24.

has been shaped by a continual displacement of the early childbearing model (concentration of first births in the age interval 20–25) with a new one in which reproductive careers begin later in life (in the late twenties or early thirties).

Figure 7-2: Extramarital Births in Bulgaria (% of all live births), 1960–2006

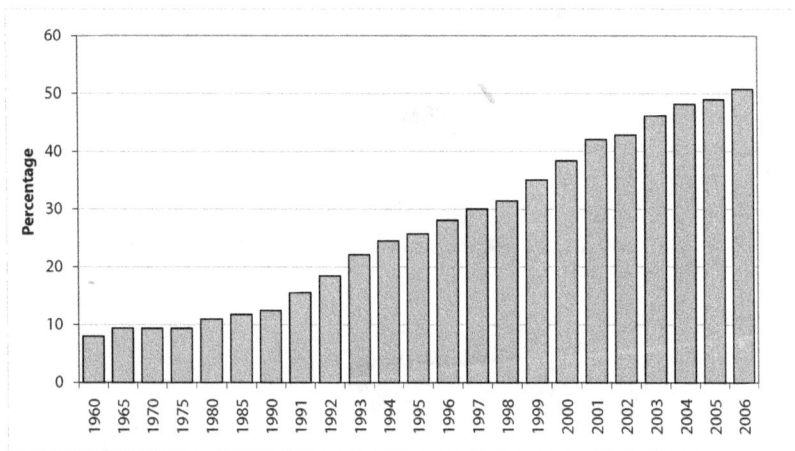

Source: Statistical Yearbook. Population, Sofia: National Statistical Institute, 2007, p. 29.

The destabilization of the previously dominating fertility regime in the country has also
been facilitated by a trend of dissociation between entry into marriage and becoming a parent as interrelated life course events. Indicative for the changing behaviours,
norms and values associated with marital parenthood is the remarkable increase of
extramarital births witnessed since the beginning of the 1990s. During the initial period
of political changes in Bulgaria, the percentage of extramarital births was 12.4% of all
live births. It was recently found that more than 50% of newborn children in Bulgaria
are raised in non-marital settings.[3] This trend is an exemplary behavioural manifesta-
tion of the changing familistic views and values of the new generations beginning the
most active part of their demographic lives in the post-socialist period in Bulgaria.

The causes of the new reproductive behavioural patterns in the country are diverse.
In the initial period, the worsened economic situation was the leading cause of postponement and reduction of fertility. However, in the later stages, when the political
and economic situation gradually stabilized, the changes in individual views and values towards family and parenthood became the leading cause of the new patterns
of reproductive behaviour.

---

3   Statistical Yearbook. Population, Sofia: National statistical Institute, 2007, p. 29.

From a demographic point of view, the recent transformations in the country's reproductive profile can be considered part of the Second Demographic Transition, which started in the early 1990s in Bulgaria. The postponement of childbearing, the reduction of fertility below population replacement level and the increasing number of children born and raised in non-marital settings are core elements of the new demographic transition. This profound demographic transformation is not limited to post-socialist countries, however; it is also unfolding across the rest of Europe.

The concept of the Second Demographic Transition (SDT), which will serve as the theoretical framework of this chapter, was introduced by R. Lesthaeghe and D. van de Kaa in the second half of the 1980s.[4] According to them, the changing demographics in north-western Europe starting at the end of the 1960s marked the beginning of a new demographic transition whose core elements included the emergence of sub-replacement fertility levels and the spread of non-marital forms of interpersonal unions.

Lesthaeghe and van de Kaa claim that the SDT was triggered by the fundamental value changes that emerged in the social setting of the post-industrial economy.[5] The child-oriented familistic culture lost ground to individualism in late-modern societies, with marriage and parenthood competing with many other choices. Self-realization was no longer limited to marrying and starting a family.

The decrease in overall fertility levels and the increasing postponement of marriage and childbearing, together with the rise in non-marital cohabitation, one-parent families and divorces, were transformations commonly experienced by the majority of European countries after a certain point in their recent demographic developments. The SDT unfolded in several waves, producing a step-by-step integration of the different parts of the continent.[6] The first wave swept over the Scandinavian societies and the Netherlands in the late 1960s. The new family values and behaviours began to diffuse from the north to the south of the continent during the 1980s, when the Mediterranean countries showed the first signs of diversification in their familistic profiles. This was the second wave of the SDT, which gradually changed the demographic profile of southern European societies. Eastern Europe, and in particular the post-socialist countries, began to show the first signs of the SDT in the early 1990s and

---

4   Lesthaeghe, Ron / van de Kaa, Dirk: Twee Demographische Transities?, in: Lesthaeghe, Ron / van de Kaa, Dirk (eds): Bevolking: Groei en Krimp?, Deventer: van Loghnm Slaterus, 1986, pp. 9–24; van de Kaa, Dirk J.: Europe's Second Demographic Transition, Population Bulletin, 1987 (Vol. 42), No. 1, Washington D. C.: Population Reference Bureau.

5   Lesthaeghe, Ron: The Second Demographic Transition in Western Countries. An Interpretation, in: Mason, Karen O. / Jesen, An-Magritt (eds): Gender and Family in Industrialized Countries, Oxford: Claredon Press, 1995, pp. 17–62; van de Kaa, Dirk: Postmodern Fertility Preferences. From Changing Value Orientations to New Behavior, in: Bulatao, Rudolfo / Casterline, John (eds): Global Fertility Transition, suppl. to Vol. 27 of Population and Development Review, New York/ NY: Population Council, 2001, pp. 290–331.

6   Van de Kaa, Dirk J.: Europe's Second Demographic Transition, Population Bulletin, 1987 (Vol. 42), No. 1, Washington D. C.: Population Reference Bureau.

formed the third wave of the process. This continent-wide transition thus continues to shape the demographic face of the global age in Europe.

In this chapter we will explore the normative aspect of the changing demographic profile of contemporary Bulgarian society by focusing on the shifting values, norms and perceptions regarding the ideal age for a woman or man to become a parent. On the one hand, the change of the reproductive ideals and norms in society can be considered a main driver of the rapid diffusion and social legitimization of the new behavioural phenomena related to parenthood. On the other hand, the changes in the subjective norms and ideals related to the temporal organization of one's life course with respect to reproduction and family formation also constitute an indicator for the future development of fertility trends in Bulgaria and their convergence to the increasing global demographic tendencies of de-standardization of individual life realization course.

7.2. Data and Methods

In the next part of the chapter we will focus on the changes in attitude with respect to the ideal age to become a parent for a woman or man in Bulgaria. This indicator has recently been discussed in the demographic literature as a proxy of social norms and personal values related to the temporal organization of individual life trajectories.

For the purposes of the analysis, the European Social Survey dataset for Bulgaria (N=1400) has been utilized. The survey was conducted in 2006. It is representative for the population above the age of 15. The survey has a special module of questions aiming to reveal individual perceptions and attitudes towards fundamental events and transitions in life such as becoming a parent, entering into marriage, getting a divorce, etc. The module integrating these topics covers special groups of selected individuals. In particular, the original sample of the population has been divided into two sub-samples and then the selected individuals responded to questions covering attitudes and perceptions towards either women's or men's life courses in terms of family formation and parenthood. Splitting the sample enables us to study the reproductive ideals and norms for women and men separately; the division is important because the ideal age of parenthood substantially differs across gender. The main limitation of the dataset is that the sub-division of the sample decreases the number of individuals in the studied population and thus precludes the application of more complicated statistical procedures.

To pin down perceptions and ideals regarding the most appropriate time to become a parent, we used the question 'In your opinion, what is the ideal age for a girl or woman to become a mother?' and the corresponding variant for men – 'In your opinion, what is the ideal age for a boy or man to become a father?'. In the original dataset it is scaled as a continuous variable. We treated the answers 'I do not know' and 'There is no appropriate time for this' as missing values and excluded them from the analysis for two reasons. Although it could be argued that these responses constitute important information on the changing perceptions regarding the temporal organization of reproduction, we are more interested here in the particular time-framing of the transition to parenthood in one's life course. The second reason for excluding these responses is more technical and relates to the fact that a very low percentage of the sampled population chose these answers. This means that the participants in our study had relatively clear perceptions, views and values regarding the most appropriate time to become a parent in men's or women's lives.

Table 7-1:   Descriptive Statistics of the Ideal Age for a Woman or Man to Become a Parent

	N	Range	Min.	Max.	Mean	Standard deviation	Variance	Skewness	Kurtosis
Ideal age for a woman to become a mother	598	17	16	33	23.74	2.78	7.72	-0.03	-0.20
Ideal age for a man to become a father	632	27	18	45	26.42	3.17	11.83	0.38	0.19

Source: European Social Survey, own calculations.

The descriptive statistics of the variables reflecting the ideal age to become a parent for the two sexes are presented in Table 7-1. It is clear that from a comparative perspective the ideal age to become a parent for men and women in Bulgaria is still closely associated with the previously dominating pattern of early childbearing. The variance within the group responding to the question about the ideal age of parenthood for women is slightly lower. This suggests that there is a greater degree of homogeneity in the respondents' perceptions regarding the ideal childbearing age for females.

In order to identify the main factors influencing the individuals' perceptions regarding the ideal age for women and men to become parents, we ran separate logistic regressions for the two sub-samples. In particular, the direction of influence was studied in order to reveal whether particular socio-demographic characteristics are more closely associated with strong preferences for the previously existing model of early childbearing, or if they in fact facilitate the emerging new pattern of reproduction later in life.

For the purposes of the analysis, the dependent variable in each of the models was split into two categories covering different perceptions towards men's and women's ideal age for parenthood. In particular, the calculated means of the dependent variables in the two sub-samples were used as cut-points to delineate the categories that reflect contrasting age patterns of fertility in Bulgaria. The following groups were created:

Ideal age for a woman to become a mother:
- The first category covers the interval from the lowest age to 24 – that is, below the sample mean. It reflects reproductive perceptions and ideals that are closely associated with the model of early childbearing.
- The second category covers the interval from age 25 to the highest fertile age of women mentioned by the respondents. It is interpreted as reflecting the subjective preferences that lay the ground for the new patterns of postponed childbearing in Bulgaria.

Ideal age for a man to become a father:
- The first interval ranges from the lowest age to 26 (below the sample mean). It is associated with subjective perceptions supporting more traditional types of reproductive behaviours strongly focused on early parenthood.
- The second interval ranges from age 27 to the highest age mentioned by the respondents. It is interpreted as reflecting the subjective preferences of those individuals who create a permissive subjective environment for the diffusion of the new patterns of reproductive behaviour.

The independent variables that have been studied for their influence on the individuals' reproductive ideals include various socio-demographic characteristics. The impact of the chosen variables has already been empirically studied and discussed in the literature. In particular, we tested the impact of education, number of children, gender, age, income, place of residence, marital status and membership in an ethnic minority. After running several models, we present here the most informative and statistically robust ones.

7.3.   Results and Discussion

The two models run to determine the respondents' estimation of the ideal age to become a parent for women and men in Bulgaria reveal that education exercises a significant impact on individual preferences towards early or postponed parenthood. The odds of choosing a later ideal reproduction age for either men or women significantly increases among the respondents with higher education levels in comparison to the group with lower levels. This result shows that the educational differentials have a strong influence on the individuals' perceptions regarding the timing of parenthood. The people with higher education levels tend to start their reproductive careers later in life, and accordingly, they tend to express stronger preferences for later reproduction.

Like education, the respondents' socio-economic status accounts for significant differences in the personal reproductive ideals and norms. The individuals who belong to medium or high income groups are more likely to choose a higher ideal age of motherhood than those who belong to low income groups. The same relation holds true with respect to the ideal age of fatherhood.

Table 7-2:   Result of Binary Logistic Regressions

Independent variables	Independent variable Ideal age to become parent			
	Women		Men	
	16–24		18–26	
	25+		27+	
	Exp(B)	Sig.	Exp(B)	Sig.
Education Primary (ref.)		**		**
Secondary	1.054		1.648	**
Tertiary	2.421	**	2.532	**
Number of children 3+ children (ref.)		**		
No children	2.653	***	1.022	
1 child	2.661	**	1.143	
2 children	2.880	**	1.372	
Gender Woman (ref.)				
Man	0.637	**	0.663	***
Age of respondent 46+ (ref.)				**
15–25	0.875		0.384	
26–35	1.271		2.419	**
36–45	0.508	**	1.121	
Gender*Age		***		
M*15–25	0.583		2.126	
M*26–35	0.722		3.335	
M*36–45	0.207	**	1.786	
Income Low (ref.)		*		**
Medium	1.804	**	1.793	**
High	3.392	*	2.009	**
Place of residence Big city (ref.)				
Village	0.263		0.753	
Small town	0.677	**	0.646	***
Marital status Married (ref.)				**
Divorced	1.434		1.053	
Widowed	0.937		1.368	
Never married	1.347		7.131	*
Ethnic minority No (ref.)				
Yes	0.311	**	0.498	**
Constant	0.263	**	0.288	**

$* P \leq 0.001; ** P \leq 0.05; *** P \leq 0.10$

The previous reproductive history of the respondents (number of children) also produces interesting effects on the odds of holding more traditional or unconventional subjective preferences towards the ideal age for reproduction. The variable is significant when the ideal age of a woman to become a parent is concerned, whereas in the case of the men's ideal age the number of children loses its explanatory power. In comparison to those respondents who have 3 or more children, the individuals with lower parity (0, 1 or 2 children) are more likely to cite a higher ideal age for a woman to enter into parenthood. The model reveals that the ideals regarding the timing of men's reproductive lives is not so strongly shaped by past reproductive experience, whereas the perceptions regarding the timing for females are much more influenced by the past reproductive careers of the individuals.

The analysis uncovers important gender differences in the respondents' perceptions of the ideal age of parenthood. It reveals that men are less likely than women to choose a later ideal reproductive age when either motherhood or fatherhood is concerned. This result confirms that the postponement effects registered by the demographic statistics are complemented by a faster process of adjustment to the new reproductive standard by Bulgarian women.

Interestingly enough, the ideal age of parenthood for women cited by respondents does not fluctuate significantly according to age group. The respondent's age significantly influences only the perceptions about the temporal organization of men's reproductive careers. However, when gender and age are created as interaction terms, we observe significant differences regarding the ideal age for women.

In the first model without interaction terms an explanation of homogeneity across age in the norms and ideals regarding the timing of women's reproductive lives could be that on a behavioural level we observe faster adaptation of the young cohorts to the new temporal reproductive standards, while on the level of reproductive values and norms there is a certain lag in the adjustment to these new standards. However, when gender is taken in interaction with age the model uncovers that women from different age groups tend to accept the new female reproductive timing faster than men.

Marital status is another important predictor of an individual's reproductive preferences, yet its explanatory power is valid only with respect to the perceptions of men's reproductive careers. Individuals who have never been married are much more likely to support a higher age of fatherhood than those who are or have been married. We do not observe statistically significant differences among the categories created on the basis of current marital status for women, however.

The empirical analyses uncover a very weak impact of one's place of residence on personal ideals for reproduction. Nevertheless, the models do register that people from small towns are less likely to cite a higher ideal age of parenthood than respondents living in big cities.

And finally, the empirical analysis confirms the existence of substantial differences among ethnic groups in Bulgarian society in terms of subjective orientations towards parenthood and the start of reproduction. The respondents who consider themselves as belonging to the Bulgarian ethnic group are much more likely to express a strong preference for a later start of reproductive careers for both men and women than the respondents who belong to some of the ethnic minorities in Bulgaria (mainly the Turkish and Roma populations).

7.4. Conclusion

The analysis reveals the influence of the various socio-economic and demographic variables on individual perceptions, ideals and attitudes regarding the temporal organization of Bulgarian men's and women's reproductive lives. In particular, people with higher incomes and education levels tend to express stronger preferences towards having children later in life. The research that has already been done confirms that in many empirical cases, high status groups tend to postpone family formation and reproduction due to prolonged time spent on their careers and education. Our analysis reveals that this empirical correlation is also valid in current Bulgarian society.

The variables of gender, ethnicity, number of children and marital status also exert a strong influence on respondents' conceptions of the ideal age for parenthood. In terms of generational differences, Bulgarian society is still relatively homogeneous. However, its subjective l profile is much more diversified when viewed through the prism of gender and ethnic divisions. In terms of gender differences Bulgarian women show faster acceptance and stronger preferences towards the new model of a later start to reproduction.

The general conclusion from the empirical analysis is that the Second Demographic Transition in Bulgaria is characterized by the gradual convergence of individuals' reproductive behaviours and norms towards the late fertility model. However, the new transition is not proceeding simultaneously on the behavioural and ideational levels. This discrepancy can be interpreted as one of the main causes for the delayed convergence between the national trends in Bulgaria and the western European processes. The late fertility model that we observe in most of the European countries is continuing to gain popularity in contemporary Bulgarian society. Thus, the Bulgarian case confirms that in terms of demographic developments, the advancement of globalization is not a homogenizing trend but proceeds as a form of 'integration towards diversity' within and between the countries. As some researchers point out,[7] the recently emerging demographic profile of Europe is multi-faceted and consists of diverse demographic landscapes that certainly will not disappear in the near future.

---

[7]   Billari, Fancesco C. / Wilson, Cris: Convergence Toward Diversity? Cohort Dynamics in the Transition to Adulthood in Contemporary Western Europe, Max Planck Institute for Demographic Research, Working Paper 2001-039, Rostock, 2001, http://ideas.repec.org/p/dem/wpaper/wp-2001-039. html

Robert Kulpa

8. Breaking the Silence. Some Thoughts About Gay and National Identities in Poland after 1989

> The researcher's goal is not to emancipate the authentic story of the narrator – none exists – but rather to expose as much as she can of the relations that influence the construction of the story that is told.[1]

> **Paradigm** [a]s used by Kuhn (1962), however, it refers to an intellectual framework comprising interrelated values, theories and assumptions, within which the search for knowledge is conducted. [...] The radical implication of this theory is that 'truth' and 'falsehood' cannot be finally established. They are only provisional judgements operating within an accepted paradigm that will, eventually, be replaced.[2]

What, then, is my truth? What is the paradigm in which this chapter is nested? My ongoing Ph.D. research, on which this article draws and from which it stems, is deeply informed by postmodern approaches to knowledge and by an experience of activism in a lesbian and gay organization in Warsaw (2001–2004). In particular, I am in debt to queer theory/ies, and their focus on de-centralizing and de-stabilizing dominant hegemonies of power, knowledge and hetero/homo-normativity.

I this chapter I will lay out the goals and reflect on my position as a researcher; then I will elaborate on national and gay identities in post-communist Poland; finally, I will conclude with closing remarks.

8.1. Goals and Positions

The transformation of Poland's political, economic, social and cultural landscape after 1989 has been ongoing for the last twenty years and has been conceptualized in various ways throughout this period.[3] Yet the trajectory of this academic work seems to be overwhelmingly written from the perspective of political sciences, economics and to a lesser extent – sociology.

---

1 Presser, Lois: Negotiating Power and narrative in Research. Implications for Feminist Methodology, in: Signs, 2005 (Vol. 30), No. 4, pp. 2067–2090, here p. 2087.
2 Heywood, Andrew: Politics, 2nd edn, London: Palgrave Macmillan, 2002, p. 20.
3 Among others, e.g. Wnuk-Lipiński, Edmund (ed.): After Communism. A multidisciplinary approach to radical social change, Warsaw: Institute of Political Studies, 1995; Gorzelak, Grzegorz: Transition, cohesion and regional policy in Central and Eastern Europe, Aldershot: Ashgate, 1999; Fischer, Sabine / Pleines, Heiko / Schröder, Hans-Henning (eds): Movements, Migrants, Marginalisation. Challenges of Societal and Political Participation in Eastern Europe and the Enlarged EU, Stuttgart: Ibidem, 2008.

What is underdeveloped is the analysis of Polish national consciousness in relation to 'freshly acquired freedom' – the struggle for 'freedom' is one of the key features of Polish national identity.[4]

Another under-examined issue in this academic context is homo/sexuality, but for different reasons. It is primarily a cultural silence that veils homo/sexuality as the invisible, hence seemingly non-existing, problem.[5]

This article, though, attempts to reconcile the two – nationalism and homo/sexuality in post-1989 Poland. In particular, I will focus on identities, their national and gay embodiments and reconfigurations. As the title of this chapter suggests, it is an assemblage of thoughts, ideas, and some conceptualizations and unfinished analytical attempts – rather than the coherent, linear narrative of academic articles to which we are used. There are two reasons for such a 'fragmented' construction.

Since the process of post-1989 transformation is neither finished nor stabilized – it is hardly possible to construct a finite reflection that would also, by means of its centralized and 'coherent' form, give the impression that it is possible to cram it into one article.

The second stems from my theoretical perspective. In a diverse world with multiplied stances and perspectives of what might constitute 'a truth' (but not 'The Truth'), there is not much more that one can do (even if one claims to occupy the privileged position of 'academic') except to collect notes, snippets, ideas, little sticky notes of knowledge(s). But this is not the only available form of writing/theorizing. Far from claiming any universalistic position, I want to deploy an attempt to write about something that is still an ongoing process, the process of which I am myself a part – as someone born in Poland, but often denying national affiliation, yet still feeling quite 'Polish', as a non-straight-identified man, sometimes gay, sometimes queer, sometimes 'passing for straight' man, etc. – and something that seems to be too overwhelmingly rich and complicated to escape the framework of single-articled articulation.

Additionally, inspired by the feminist epistemologies highlighting the need of situatedness and self-reflexivity in the process of knowledge production,[6] I am writing myself into this text by using various (grammatical) forms of narration, as well

---

4   See e.g. Shallcross, Bożena (ed.): Framing the Polish Home. Postwar Cultural Constructions of Hearth, Nation, and Self, Athens/OH: Ohio University Press, 2002; or Auer, Stefan: Liberal Nationalism in Central Europe, London: Routledge, 2004.
5   See: Ritz, German: Nić w labiryncie pożądania. Gender i płeć w literaturze polskiej od romantyzmu do postmodernizmu, Warsaw: Wiedza Powszechna, 2002; and Sypniewski, Zbyszek / Warkocki, Błażej (eds): Homophobia po Polsku, Warsaw: Sic!, 2004.
6   See for example Haraway, Donna: Modest_witness@Second_Millenium, New York/NY: Routledge, 1996; Signs, 2005 (Vol. 30), No. 4 (special issue); Viesweswaran, Kamala: In Fictions of Feminist Ethnography, Minneapolis/MN: University of Minnesota Press, 1994 or Anzaldua, Gloria (ed.): Making Face, Making Soul (Haciendo Cras), San Francisco/CA: Aunt Lute Books, 1990.

as by drawing on my own experiences and conceptualizations, which now serve as inspiration and a valuable source of information.

8.2. National Identities

Although various authors focus on different aspects of Polish national identity,[7] the core features would be: (1) the strong presence of religion (especially the Catholic Church), martyrdom and victimhood; (2) the multi-ethnic society until the end of the WWII, and ethnic homogeneity after; (3) Polish relations with Jews and with Russians and Germans; (4) the exclusionist social attitude fuelled by a sense of inferiority and superiority to neighbouring countries.

Below I will suggest that the post-1989 situation complicates the relationship between these four national features and reality. However, I do not want to say that these identified elements have no relevancy. Conversely, they are of great importance, e.g. in the light of rising populist, nationalist and conservative parties, or in cases of discussions about Poland's place in the European Union. The preliminary analysis of discourses of 'liberal'/progressive and 'conservative'/nationalist voices[8] points towards the fact that what is at stake is the different understanding of what constitutes the paradigm of 'Polishness'. Therefore, the critique I offer aims to displace the above-mentioned core elements, and urges readers to re-think and re-conceptualize the notion of national identity in post-1989 Poland.

***

Religiosity used to shape the morals and ethics of everyday life, forming a central feature of Polish national identity. Across years and centuries, the relatively independent Catholic Church helped to transmit other cultural values, which would otherwise have been in danger of extinction (such as during the partitioning period 1795–1918)[9]. Today, however, Poles no longer perceive religion as the most important facet in their everyday lives.

---

7   Amongst many such authors see e.g. Janion, Maria: Do Europy tak, ale razem z naszymi umarłymi, Warsaw: Sic!, 2000; Young, Mitchell / Zuelow, Eric / Sturm, Andreas (eds): Nationalism in a Global Era. The Persistence of Nations, London: Routledge 2007; Auer, Stefan: Liberal nationalism in Central Europe, New York/NY, London: Routledge, 2004; Spohn, Willfried / Atsuko, Ichijo (ed.): Entangled Identities. National and European Identity, Aldershot: Ashgate, 2005.

8   I have looked at content of the main daily papers: 'Gazeta Wyborcza' and 'Rzeczpospolita' with occasional scanning of Catholic/nationalistic paper 'Nasz Dziennik' across several years, particularly around such moments as the EU negotiations and enlargements, workers' strikes, same-sex partnership proposals and claims of some small German and private associations for 'land repossession' as compensation for post-war forced relocation.

9   Auer, Stefan: Liberal Nationalism in Central Europe, London: Routledge, 2004, pp. 68–70.

Sociological analysis of Polish religiousness shows that a great amount of Poles treat religious truths and teachings selectively. Occasional spectacular gestures, like mass pilgrimages [...] are not always accompanied by the amelioration of religious life.[10]

On the other hand, what was once a 'religious aspect' in the national tradition has marched into contemporary politics arm in arm with the Solidarity workers' movement as '*The* Catholic Church'. The institutionalization of religion is not a new phenomenon, however. From at least 1795 until 1989, it was the Catholic religion that bound people together, to the extent that Catholic values and Polish norms were inextricably intertwined (the fact that Poland's past oppressors, the Russians and the Germans, were primarily Orthodox and Protestant, respectively, made it even easier to unite Catholicism and Polishness as 'one'). When (neo)liberal democracy was inaugurated in Poland after 1989, new, (neo)liberal values came into play, succeeding in pushing aside religious tenets of public life. That was when the Catholic Church 'reinvented' and re-established itself in public life – not through values, but as an institutionalized, political actor.

*The primacy of the collective over the individual (**Martyrology**)* in the national ideology has taken various shapes, mainly the form of fighting with a (real or imagined) 'Oppressor'. Prior to 1989 – during the partitioning period, and then under communism – suppressing personal happiness for the sake of 'The Polish Nation' was established as the core value. The romantic idea of Poland as the Christ of nations, sacrificing itself at the altar of the world's freedom, exemplifies the myth of injustice and victimhood that has long been a part of the national ego.[11] 'Tearful', 'over-angelic' and 'full of martyrdom' Polish Messianism[12] had to yield space to other problems that came with the abolition of communism in 1989. Overall, the stress after 1989 came to rest on the 'state/citizen' pairing, as opposed to the earlier 'Poland/nation' duo. This represented a shift from the 'cultural' to the 'civic', where 'civic' identity came to play a greater role, in line with the requirements of the newly formed (neo)liberal democracy. For example, the Solidarity trade union was wrecked by its own members in the first fully free parliamentary elections of 1991. Small party interests won over unitary politics. Individual/ small interest group perspectives won over communitarian/national ones.

Ethnic diversity. The Commonwealths of Poland and Lithuania of the pre-partition period and the Second Republic (1918–1939) had minority populations of more

---

10   Brzoza, Czesław / Sowa, Andrzej Leon: Wielka Historia Polski, Vol. V, 2003, Cracow, Warsaw: Fogra, Świat Książki, p. 793.

11   Janion, Maria: Wobec zła, Chotomów: Verba, 1989; Janion, Maria: Do Europy tak, ale razem z naszymi umarłymi, Warsaw: Sic!, 2000; Zubrzycki, Genevieve: The Cross, the Madonna, and the Jew. Persistent Symbolic Representations of the Nation in Poland, in: Young, Mitchell / Zuelow, Eric / Sturm, Andreas (eds): Nationalism in a Global Era. The Persistence of Nations, London: Routledge 2007, pp. 131–151.

12   Szrett, Józef: The Valley Between the Mountains, in: Kostrzewa, Robert (ed.): Between East and West. Writings From Kultura, New York/NY: Hill and Wang, 1990, pp. 25–38, here p. 36.

than 30%. Ultimately, Polish culture was founded on these multiethnic roots, which were bonded together by the civic political idea(lism)s of unity.[13] The post-war disappearance of ethnic minorities has given Poles the false impression (one based on ethnic representation, which omits non-ethnic and 'other' identities and attitudes) that Polish society is a homogeneous organism. This erroneous conviction systematically forms a background for conservative attitudes, especially in the context of 'modern' problems in Polish society, such as xenophobia and discrimination.[14]

Presence of Jews and the East/West divide. Until WWII, the Jewish minority living in Poland comprised a significant 10% of the overall population; the Shoah and events of March 1968 reduced the number of Jews to a fraction of that percentage. Today, many commentators point out that there is a functional parallel between Jews and gays, i.e. that of a scapegoat. It has been said that homophobia is the anti-Semitism of the twenty-first century.[15] However, even though homophobia and anti-Semitism may bear structural and functional resemblances, they still encompass huge differences requiring further assessment.

Finally, *the East/West divide* has seemingly faded. After 1989, Poland entered into the world processes of globalization, which lessened the divide. Moreover, its accession to the EU in 2004 is often read as the final answer for the question of to which tradition Poland belongs. Still, many remain dubious. This doubt is reflected in the relationship with the neighbouring countries of Germany and Russia. Poles feel inferior to the former and superior to the latter. The prominent Polish intellectual Jan Józef Lipski critiques this duality of the 'Polish soul', concluding that the Polish attitude is 'grotesque' and 'pitiful'[16].

8.3. Gay Identities

The pre-communist era was characterized by the superiority of the nation over the individual and infused with patriarchal (i.e. heterosexualized) gender roles (mothers and warriors).[17] During communism, primacy was given to the collective body of the citizenry, and heterosexuality was present as an implicit rule (reproduction as the key duty in the service of (re)building the country/nation). In general, I would then suggest that the pre-communist and communist eras were both characterized by (1) disregard

---

13 Walicki, Andrzej: Intellectual Elites and the Vicissitudes of Imagined Nation in Poland, in: East European Politics and Societies, 1997 (Vol. 11), No. 2, pp. 227–253, here p. 233.
14 Umińska (Keff), Bożena: Barykady. Kroniki obsesyjne, Cracow: Wydawnictwo eFKa, 2006.
15 See works of Bożena Umińska, Agnieszka Graff or Adam Ostolski.
16 Lipski, Jan Józef: Two Fatherlands. Two Patriotisms, in: Kostrzewa, Robert (ed.): Between East and West. Writings from Kultura, New York/NY: Hill and Wang, 1990, pp. 52–71, here p. 60.
17 Siemieńska, Renata: Factors shaping conceptions of women's and men's roles in Poland, in: Domsch, Michel / Ladwig, Desire (eds): Reconciliation of Family and Work in Eastern European Countries, Berlin: Peter Lang, 2000.

for the individual, with no allowance for pluralism; (2) a lack of openness to 'Otherness' (often identified with physical geography and liminal spots: East and/or West, 'outside Poland', expulsion/defecation from the inside of the body/nation, etc.); and (3) the strong existence of resistance – resistance against the oppressor, something outside; and internal resistance within the country/culture against the compulsory system of thinking, behaving, consuming, etc.

According to German Ritz, one of the most significant aspects of Polish culture around homo/sexuality is silence and the conformity of cultural life. Homosexuality occupied an unclear position in the cultural imagination, most often (if at all) presented through the lenses of art or the excessive aristocratic (bourgeois) lifestyle. Ritz recognizes differences in the development of Western and Polish social structures/hierarchies (sexuality as a Western middle-class commodity), and suggests that it could be another reason why the absence/presence of homosexuality in Poland is different from Western societies. Sypniewski and Warkocki also follow this path, pointing towards the direction that the 'unspoken' status of homosexuality does not mean 'non-existence'[18].

Overall, Polish literature on homosexuality has a predominantly general, or indeed, very specialized character, focusing on the analysis of one event or film or other cultural artefacts. Furthermore, many authors refer to and often base their work on Western lesbian and gay studies and theories in an attempt to familiarize Polish readers with this body of work.[19]

What I would like to underscore in this chapter is the fact that before 1989, the notion or concept of 'gay identity' did not exist in Polish society. Changes ignited by the Solidarity movement in 1980, with their culmination in 1989 of the rebellious overthrow of communist rule, soon inaugurated the arrival of a (neo)liberal democracy. This brought about not only a change of economic and political system, but also serious shifts in the structure of society generally and in the system of social values. One of the major goals of the Solidarity movement was new legislation that would enable self-organization in civil society. This legal change allowed homosexual groups (that had started to organize themselves by 1987/88) to 'legalize' their existence and to formalize their structures as organizations. In June 1990, the monthly magazine 'Inaczej' arrived on the scene, quickly becoming the dominant publication serving

---

18   Ritz, German.: Nić w labiryncie pożądania. Gender i płeć w literaturze polskiej od romantyzmu do postmodernizmu, Warsaw: Wiedza Powszechna, 2002; and Sypniewski, Zbyszek / Warkocki, Błażej (eds): Homophobia po Polsku, Warsaw: Sic!, 2004.

19   See e.g. Basiuk, Tomasz / Ferens, Dominika / Sikora, Tomasz (eds): Odmiany odmieńca. Mniejszosciowe orientacje seksualne w perspektywie gender / A queer mixture. Gender perspectives on minority sexual identities, Katowice: Wydawnictwo Naukowe Śląsk, 2002; Kochanowski, Jacek: Fantazmat zróżnicowany. Socjologiczne studium przemian tożsamości gejów, Cracow: Universitas, 2004; Mizielińska, Joanna: (De)Konstrukcje kobiecosci. Podmiot feminizmu a problem wykluczenia, Gdańsk: Słowo/Obraz Terytoria, 2004, among others.

the homosexual community for the next ten years. The preliminary analysis of the early issues of this magazine along with my own engagement in the Lambda LGBT organization have helped me to pose an initial set of opening suggestions concerning homosexual people, their constructions of identity and the formation of a new public sphere in post-communist Poland.

I begin with the hypothesis that although homosexuality was present in the Polish cultural and social *imaginarium* (albeit unnamed) before 1989, it was the (neo)liberal democratic shift in 1989 that had enabled (or made?) homosexual people to become 'gay' and 'lesbian'. In other words, I see the emergence and formation of a 'gay community' as the formation of 'gay identity'. And once homosexuals acquired a 'new' name along with an identity based on sexuality, the process of consciousness-raising and self-organizing led them towards the struggle for greater visibility in the public sphere. Of course, this is not a linear process and this description in no way insists on such consecutiveness. As had happened thirty years earlier in the Western metropolis, once homosexuals began to dare to speak 'their' name and break the cultural bond of silence and shatter the unspoken acceptance of non-existence, the question was whether maintaining and enlarging visibility had also become the major issue for the gay community. Or, put another way, if a sphere of homosexual people activated within the sphere of civil society would centralize itself around the notion of being gay and lesbian – i.e. around gay or lesbian identity?

The second suggestion concerns the impact of the gay community, built around the gay identity, on the public sphere in Poland. As noted above, 'acquiring a name' for homosexual desire and labelling it 'gay' was an act of shattering the culturally sanctioned public silence. My presumption is that the following struggle for visibility (i.e. existence) as the intervention into public space and consciousness must have had some consequences not only for the gay community, but also for mainstream society. It has challenged traditional Polish values, such as the subordination of the individual to the nation, religiousness and obedience to the teachings of the Catholic Church, patriarchal gender roles and the disregard of foreign cultures. Instead, 'gay people' opted for the 'modern European' set of values: individualism, pluralism, secular ethics, and freedom of choice of (gender and sexual) social behaviour. In my view, this clash, as represented in public debates in the media, legislative initiatives over the issue of discrimination, or social campaigns, is one of the main problems of Poland's post-1989 culture, and it becomes very clear when we consider the role of the EU and the Catholic Church in recent years.

8.4. The EU and the Catholic Church (CC)

The CC is a social and cultural institution that evolved on the bedrock of Poland's traditionally religious society. It grew in strength during communism, even though circumstances were not conducive. It was possible because the Church linked itself with the opposition, successfully merging the notion of resistance with religiousness.[20] Nonetheless, at the beginning of 1990s the Church seriously damaged its own credibility due to its involvement in politics around the abortion debate.[21] Both power holders, the EU and the CC, have been present in Polish culture throughout the last twenty years. Homo/sexuality (but not exclusively) was 'the issue' that helped to crystallize the conflict of interests between the two. Moreover, it escalated exchange and power dynamics in order to dominate/hegemonize and re-appropriate the space of political, cultural and social life. The clash between the EU and the Church was, and is, about values, attitudes towards sexuality (and gender), and the meaning of 'Polishness'.

The Church pushes tradition and does not recognize changing social reality as being important to progress: it is instead bent upon renewing the old national paradigm. The 'neutral' and pro-diversity discourses of EU institutions and the proclamation of positive (even joyful) and pro-active attitudes towards the future clashed with the martyrological, past-oriented, religious account of social relations offered by the CC. Sexuality became one of the most important battles, seen and promoted as the celebration of the individual vs. reproduction of a nation; the freedom to choose vs. obedience.

8.5. Conclusions

The CC (as observed in the Catechism), the EU (as in legislatives and directives) and the gay community (in their pledges) agree with each other in one respect: they understand the existence of sexual identities and public ignorance about them as an opportunity to communicate their views about social, cultural and political spheres. The transition period is a time of tensions between national and supranational, local and global, gay and Polish, etc. Each side advocates seemingly different interests, but this conflict may be understood as a failed attempt to communicate because of the 'incompatible languages' used by each side. If the Church safeguards the traditional paradigm, it may see the (neo)liberal EU as a threat to the national identity and culture. Although the Church did not object to EU enlargement officially, the conflicting issues are apparent when considering e.g. feminism, abortion and homosexuality. The Church would clearly prefer to silence these issues and have them put back into the

---

20   Chrypinski, Vincent C.: Church and Nationality in Postwar Poland, in: Ramet, Pedro (ed.): Religion and Nationalism in Soviet and East European Politics, London, Durham: Duke University Press, 1989, pp. 241–263, here p. 241.

21   Kramer, Anne-Marie: Gender, Nation, and Abortion Debate in the Polish Media, in: Tolz, Vera / Booth, Stephanie (eds): Nation and Gender in Contemporary Europe, Manchester: Manchester University Press, 2005, pp. 130–148.

'intimate/private' sphere, while the EU raises them in its directives, law enforcements and official statements.

8.6. Identities

Finally, let me write something about the general perspective I hold on identities and the process of identification.

According to Richard Jenkins, the etymology of the word *identity* reveals its core notion: *sameness* and *difference*; thus the two determine all other aspects. 'Identity' as the outcome of a process of *identification* with (same) or against (different) something/someone else is thus a matter of constant *becoming*, not stable acquisition.[22] Additionally, the process points towards the categories of *temporality* and *processuality*. Finally, identity provides a set of rules of *moral and ethical conduct*, i.e. establishes the path, trajectory and signposts indicating the way to behave/live.[23] All other issues are built upon those basic characteristics and significantly depend on the wider epistemological perspectives.

An interesting approach to the understanding of identities/identifications can be found in the body of literature, social activism and everyday life termed as 'queer'. My own practice of queer rejects essentialism (e.g. sexuality as a biological fact). The queer practice of my everyday life convinces me that there are no stable 'identities', but only temporal arrangements, constantly moving, re-negotiating their own position(s) and notion(s). Identity-forming elements intersect, combine, collide with each other, and therefore it is not possible to freeze this process in one stable category of sexual identity, national identity, or any other kind of identity.[24] Identities are always multiple and of equal status, meaning that their importance and/or status and various hieratical configurations are the effects of the constant process of prioritization that a person makes (according to the situational context) and are not inherently valuable. Because of this dramatic diversification and pluralization, identities should therefore have a pragmatic dimension and are not to be valued on their own. Finally, such a perspective calls for more reflection on our own positioning – places we occupy as activists, researchers, politicians, housewives, employees, readers, etc.[25]

***

This contribution was meant to present several issues that appear on the researcher's way to studying Polish national and gay identities. Beginning by emphasizing the need for situatedness in the process of any knowledge production and the impossibility

---

22   Jenkins, Richard: Social Identity, London: Routledge, 1996, p. 4.
23   Poole, Ross: Nation and Identity, London: Routledge, 1999, p. 70.
24   Ibid., p. 70.
25   See interview with Judith Butler in Mizielińska's, Joanna: Płeć/Ciało/Seksualność. Od feminizmu do teorii queer, Krakòw: Universitas, 2006.

of ultimate statements, I have pointed to 'fragmentation' as a possible approach to thinking and writing about the mentioned issues. I suggested therefore that the article's 'claims' can be only read as a collection of thoughts, ideas and suggestions, rather than as a finished analysis. Hope you have enjoyed it! (P.S. Is 'joy' a category that suits academic writing and reading?)

Anna Wylegała

9. Memory, Memories and Rootedness. A New Polish Community in a Formerly German Town

9.1. Introduction

The aim of this chapter is to present the process of change in the fields of local historical memory and local identity in western Poland.[1] The 'Regained Lands', the current north-western territories of Poland, were populated almost exclusively by Germans until the war. After the war, as result of international decrees, those territories were incorporated into the new communist Polish state. Over 3.5 million Germans were forced to leave their homes, while another 3.5 million had already left at the end of the war.[2] In return, over 1.7 million inhabitants of the former eastern territories of Poland, which were incorporated into the USSR, settled in the region.[3] Other large groups of settlers were people from central and western Poland, who decided to move in search of a better life, land and work.

The 'Regained Lands' became a kind of social laboratory during the communist period. Completely new communities were created in their social vacuum. People coming from various regions and with various experiences were brought together and forced to build new local communities. Moreover, they were subjected to strong communist propaganda which was aimed at creating the conviction that there was an 'immemorial' affiliation of those territories to Polish culture and statehood.[4] Topics such as expulsion of the Germans and former 'small homelands' left in the east were forbidden. Two generations of inhabitants in the new western and northern territories of Poland were brought up in a situation where the entire community's historical memory and the memories of their parents and grandparents had been repressed. For those communities, the fall of communism meant more than important external changes and political, economical and social transformation. It also represented a release of the repressed memory and created the necessity of building a new one in

---

1   The research was conducted thanks to support of the Center of Urban History of East Central Europe, Lviv, Ukraine.

2   Madajczyk, Piotr: Niemcy polscy 1944–1989, Warsaw: Oficyna Nowa, 2001; Frantzioch, Marion: Socjologiczne aspekty problemu wypędzenia Niemców, in: Orłowski, Hubert / Sakson, Andrzej (eds): Utracona ojczyzna. Przymusowe wysiedlenia, deportacje i przesiedlenia jako wspólne doświadczenie, Poznań: Instytut Zachodni, 1996, pp. 143–170.

3   Urban, Thomas: Utracone ojczyzny. Wypędzenia Niemców i Polaków w XX w., Warsaw: Czytelnik, 2007.

4   Sakson, Andrzej: Niemcy w świadomości społecznej Polaków, in: Wolff-Pawęska, Anna (ed.): Polacy wobec Niemców. Z dziejów kultury politycznej Polski 1945–1989, Poznań: Instytut Zachodni, 1993, pp. 408–429.

a completely changed situation; a situation characterized by the availability of information, the neutrality of the state, the presence of former inhabitants of the region coming to visit it and – of equal importance – the opportunity to visit one's former 'small homeland'.

In this chapter, I will present the preliminary results of my research conducted in a small town in north-western Poland (named Kreuz before the war, currently Krzyż). Before the war, Kreuz/Krzyż was a German border station on the frontier with Poland. It was populated almost exclusively by Germans; Poles lived only in the neighbouring villages. At the end of the war, most of the male population had already been killed on the front or were in Prisoner-of-War camps, while the remainder, together with the women, children and elderly, fled to Germany. Those who stayed were deported during the first post-war years. Those who arrived to these empty towns were mainly Poles deported from the former Polish eastern territories, emigrants from central Poland, settlers from neighbouring Polish villages and a small group of party nomenclature.

This research, which I have been working on since May 2007, anticipates the use of a cross-generational approach, namely interviews in families with representatives of each generation. So far, twenty interviews with the elder inhabitants of the town have been conducted (interviewees aged seventy-one to ninety-three, among them seven women and eight men), as well as ten interviews with representatives of the middle generation (five men, five women, aged thirty-nine to sixty-one) and several less structured talks with members of the younger generation. The methodological approach follows oral history standards and the technique of the biographical in-depth, semi-directed interview.[5] At the same time, the research includes participative observation while staying in the town for longer periods of time, taking part in local celebrations of state, religious and local holidays, and non-biographical interviews with local leaders (teachers, town council members, priests, librarians).

The goal of this research is to answer the question about the current shape of the local historical memory in various generations of the community. My understanding of the notion of historical memory follows the works of Halbwachs and Szacka.[6] However, adding the 'local' before 'historical' indicates that the subject of the research is remembering a local, not national or any other more widely understood past. What interests me is what and how the inhabitants of Krzyż remember and know about their town history and its former inhabitants. How do people evaluate the political and territorial changes since 1945 which led to their settlement of the 'Regained Lands' today? What is the image of the civilian German population encountered on those territories

5   Thompson, Paul: The Voice of the Past. Oral History, Oxford: Oxford University Press, 1978; Helling, I. K.: Metoda badań biograficznych, in: Włodarek, J. / Ziółkowski, M. (eds): Metoda biograficzna w socjologii, Warsaw, Poznań: Wydawnictwo PWN, 1990, pp. 13–38.
6   Halbwachs, Maurice: Społeczne ramy pamięci, Warsaw: Wydawnictwo PWN, 1969; Szacka, Barbara: Czas przeszły, pamięć, mit, Warsaw: Wydawnictwo Naukowe Scholar, 2006.

in 1945? What is the attitude toward Germans today, especially when they come to visit their former homes? To what extent do people of various generations feel at home in this town, where before the war there were neither Poles nor Polish culture?

9.2. The Elder Generation

In my contribution, I will focus mainly on the interviews with the oldest generation since the current stage of research for this part of the material is the most complete one. The oldest generation is the only one which personally encountered the previous inhabitants of the town in their place of residence and who were witnesses to the transformation of the German town into a Polish one. In their case, one should talk not only about collectively and socially understood memory, but first and foremost about personal memories, later influenced by collective imagination; and probably because the war and first post-war years in Krzyż are those people's most important biographical experience, it seems that the influence of official propaganda and collective imagination was rather marginal in this case.

The interviewees from the oldest generation are fully conscious of the German past of the town. Those who came from neighbouring Polish villages visited Krzyż before the war and thus knew it as a place from outside the borders, not Polish, but German. Also the repatriates do not have any illusions about who lived in the town before they did. Even after the Germans were completely expelled, the new settlers used things which reminded them of the former Germanness of the place every day: school notebooks left by German children, kitchen items with German inscriptions on them and German mailboxes. Additionally, both groups met the German civilian population upon arriving in Krzyż; some people even lived together with Germans for a couple of weeks or months before the latter left for the west. Interestingly, the general image of Germans is rather positive in the memories of both groups. Only one person expressed open hatred and hostility toward Germans in general. Instead, a portion of the interviewees – mostly those coming from eastern Poland – felt sympathy for the civilian population that was expelled from their houses, just as they were expelled only some time before. Several issues can explain such a positive or at least neutral attitude. First and foremost, no one, apart from the one person already mentioned, experienced serious reprisals from the Germans. Interviewees from neighbouring Polish villages were German forced labourers during the war, but they were happy to work in small family farms or workshops (where they were treated very well), rather than in the work camps or large land estates. They spent the war far away from the German atrocities and met mostly 'normal', 'average' Germans. The real war – the front experience and war damage – began for them with the arrival of the Soviet Army. For interviewees coming from the east, this was even more significant: those who were arresting, killing and displacing Poles to Siberia were Soviets, not Germans, and the Soviets were responsible for their displacement from the eastern frontier after 1945. In comparison to the Soviets, who were also perceived as barbarians and representatives of a hostile civilization, the Germans' faults seemed much smaller.[7]

Consciousness of the past of the town, however, did not make the process of adaptation to the new place much easier. None of the interviewees came to Krzyż fully voluntarily and this fact obviously influences their attitude to the town as such. Various research shows that the most successful migrations – that is, migrations which resulted in a full reconstruction of the immigrants' social structures in the new place – are voluntary migrations in which immigrants feel that they can make decisions about their own lives.[8] For the immigrants to Krzyż, it was the war which made them settle in this town and thus which changed their lives radically. For some of them, the severe economic conditions in their pre-war place of residence made them move to the empty and ruined town. The other group, the so called 'repatriates', was made to leave their former houses on the east and then forced to settle in Krzyż. For them, the process of adaptation was particularly difficult. After the displacement, they encountered totally a different environment, architecture, landscape and living conditions. The longing for the homeland left in the east and feelings of impermanence – during the first few years after the-war, a new war was expected at any moment – provided in many cases a reason to dislike the new place. People did not want to settle in seriously because they still hoped to return.

In the case of the 'Poznanians' (settlers from neighbouring villages, inhabitants of the Poznan voivodeship) the feeling of alienation was much smaller. The German style of the buildings and everyday culture were not so different from what they knew from home. However, both groups of new settlers took part in the process of 'de-Germanization' and then 'Polonization' of the town, which in the case of the repatriates was also an attempt to make the new place of living resemble the old one. For both groups, the gradual process of adaptation to the new place was more a process of establishing the community's rootedness in space than in history.[9] The space was 'domesticated' by giving new names to the streets, villages, schools, taking down German monuments and building new ones, and transforming Protestant churches

---

7 This paradox – a positive/neutral image of the Germans and a negative image of the Soviets – has been widely discussed in research dealing with repatriates' biographical narratives: Kaźmierska, Kaja: Doświadczenia wojenne Polaków a kształtowanie tożsamości etnicznej. Analiza narracji kresowych, Warsaw: Wydawnictwo IFiS PAN, 1999.

8 A useful typology of successful and unsuccessful migrations can be found in: Mach, Zdzisław: Niechciane miasta. Migracja i tożsamość społeczna, Cracow: Universitas, 1998.

9 I understand rootedness here as the 'awareness of having one's own place in the world, having special references to the past, references [of an individual] which make up his/her sense of continuation, duration in time and space'. Melchior, Małgorzata: Rootedness in place, rootedness in memory as exemplified by Polish-Jewish identity, in: Sprawy Narodowościowe, 2007 (Vol. 31), pp. 71–80.

into Catholic ones. Feelings of belonging to the community were gradually created by getting to know neighbours, new friends and through mixed marriages between people from different groups of settlers. Even though the history was known, it could not be used as a basis for local identity and a new local community because it did not belong to the group as such. To assimilate the space, its history needed to be ignored in silence.

After more than sixty years, the place has obviously ceased to be completely 'new' and 'alien'. However, the memory of the first post-war years of instability and uncertainty is still alive among the interviewees. Additionally, differences in the way certain groups of settlers identify with the town are still visible. For interviewees who came from the east, the lost homeland and the experience of displacement is still very important. Their rootedness in space is still double – in many cases their orientation in the lost space of the hometown or village in the east is at least as good as their orientation in the space of Krzyż. Moreover, the oldest generation of interviewees still divide inhabitants of the town into people from the eastern frontier and 'Poznanians', even though all of them define themselves now first and foremost as inhabitants of Krzyż.

These strong sub-identifications and vivid memories from the war (and lost homelands) do not create any challenges to the current situation. My interviewees – especially those from the eastern frontier – in no way see the post-war border changes as positive, but in their understanding there was no other solution at this time, and it is too late to change anything now. Usually, they do not visit their homelands even though it is possible today. When asked why, they answer that they do not want to see it in ruins and that it would not result in any good. However, they greet Germans coming to visit Krzyż with sympathy and understanding, somehow envying their courage to come back. It is important that among the oldest generation of my interviewees there is no fear of Germans who will 'come and take our houses' – the slogan so often used in western Poland before the referendum on EU accession. People are convinced that they are the legitimate owners of their town, and just as they do not harbour any inclinations to revenge, they are not afraid of others having them.

9.3. The Younger Generations

The younger generations – the generation born in the 1940s to 1960s and the generation born in the 1970s to 1990s – only know the war and first post-war years from family narratives, school, official propaganda (in case of the middle generation). This means that they did not directly experience the presence of other groups and cultures in their hometown's past, but through certain media transmissions. The war was not a direct experience for any of them; none of them remember Germans in Krzyż and the Germanness of the town as such. It is true that the middle generation played among the war ruins and remembers having things with German names and inscriptions from childhood. However, both the middle and youngest generation of the interviewees heard little or nothing at all about Germans in Krzyż. It was not an important topic in their families; there were no tales about living together with civilian Germans, even if their parents really experienced such coexistence before 1946.This situation was a direct consequence of the general attitude toward town history, neither hostility toward its German past, nor affirmation of it; it was simply ignored. The younger generations derived their knowledge of the town and regional history from official sources – school textbooks, official media and commemoration ceremonies on the local and state level. The middle generation in particular grew up in an atmosphere of very strong state propaganda which forced the vision of the immemorial Polishness of the 'Regained Lands' and anti-German agitation upon them. Quite often, this fostered a belief in the 'Germanization' of a small number of Poles in 'Regained Lands' before the war among the middle generation. The youngest generation, brought up at the end of the communist period or after 1989, learned history from different textbooks, where for the first time the post-war expulsion of the Germans was at least briefly mentioned. However, they repeat in part clichés about Poles who once were living in Krzyż and only afterwards were replaced by the Germans.

For the younger generation, this family history is something related, not experienced, and of course it influences their attitudes to the town where they were born as the first or second generation of new inhabitants. For those, whose parents or grandparents came to Krzyż from neighbouring Polish villages, the pre-war border is already unrecognizable. Whereas Krzyż, even though it was only ten or fifteen kilometres from their home village, was for the older generation in a foreign country before the war, for the younger interviewees it has been always part of their country. In some cases the youngest interviewees, mostly teenagers, even do not realize that Krzyż was in Germany before the war. Such ignorance is much less common among those interviewees whose parents and grandparents came to Krzyż from the eastern frontier of Poland. Most of them more or less know their family history, and are at least conscious that they have their origins in today's Ukraine or Belarus. Although the 'eastern frontier stories' were not welcome in the communist period, displacement was such a defining experience for repatriates that its memory was carefully cultivated in their families. However, even if the children and grandchildren of the repatriates know the history of their family arrival in Krzyż, it is still not their own experience. It did not change their own lives, they do not regret living here instead of in the east, and they feel no nostalgia. While talking about their friends or neighbours, they do not divide them into 'from the east' and 'from Poznan' because for them all inhabitants of Krzyż are simply from Krzyż.

While for the oldest interviewees the space needed to be 'domesticated' in order to be accepted, for the younger generation this particular space is the only one known as their 'own' from the very beginning; it does not need any changes to become familiar and safe. They do not have any feeling of alienation toward German material culture – mostly because they simply have not noticed that something was German. The architectural features which were perceived as alien and strange by their parents and grandparents are simply local and obvious to them. Interestingly, Germanness sometimes appears in the form of vocabulary and passes unnoticed: people refer to an 'after-German' building, not necessarily meaning 'belonging to the Germans before the war,' but rather, 'old, good, solidly built house, which probably needs some restoration'.

As in the case of the oldest generation, the younger interviewees build their local identity more on rootedness in space than in time. They are proud of having been born in this particular place; they value the beautiful countryside, and feel attached to the town and their neighbourhoods. However, while their parents/grandparents had to create an attachment consciously by focusing on the place and ignoring history, which at that time and in those conditions was the only way to 'domesticate' the town, for the younger interviewees the attachment is natural. They are part of the community because they were born here and thus belong here. The situation of the older generation was not as obvious.

As has already been stated, the younger interviewees' attitude towards the former Germanness of their town is quite unreflective. They are, on the whole, aware of it, but on a rather superficial level. Instead, they situate town history in the frame of the regional history of Greater Poland. Even though, Krzyż was, in fact, never part of the historical region of Greater Poland (only after the war was the adjective denoting 'Greater Poland' added to the name of the town – Krzyż Wielkopolski – as it was to many names in the 'Regained Lands'). Historical events connected with the region, for example Greater Poland's Uprisings in 1918, are important events in their history for them. It is also visible in official celebrations and commemorations. During this year's celebrations of Third of May (Polish First Constitution Day, 1794) the honour guard stood by the monument of 'The Return of the Regained Land to the Motherland' located in the centre of the town all day. The guards wore uniforms of the insurgents of 1918, who never actually fought in the area of Krzyż. As we can see, a lack of actual rootedness in time is not a problem; when it is needed, the relationship can be constructed.[10]

Younger generations of the interviewees rarely see Germans as the former inhabitants of the town; more often they treat them as neighbours from the other side of the border, potential economical partners and normal tourists. Such an attitude is mainly prevalent among the youngest people, raised in an independent Poland, and

---

10 Obviously, this recalls Hobsbawm's 'invention of tradition'. Hobsbawm, Eric / Ranger, Terence (eds): The Invention of Tradition, Cambridge: Cambridge University Press, 1983.

is quite similar to the attitude towards German in Poland in general.[11] They did not experienced the largest wave of German 'sentimental tourism' to western Poland in the seventies and hardly remember the second wave at the beginning of the nineties. Today, Germans coming to Krzyż as tourists are generally mostly normal tourists, coming to take advantage of the fresh air and beautiful countryside. Former inhabitants are already too old or, as with the Polish repatriates from the Eastern frontier, do not want to visit their lost homeland. The middle generation is somehow less enthusiastic about the Germans and the most prejudiced among all the interviewees. The oldest people were resistant to communist anti-German propaganda because of their direct contact with German civilians after the war; the youngest generation was not exposed to such an influence or was exposed to it to a very small extent; in contrast, the middle generation did not have any of those advantages and this can, in part, explain their distrust.

There is one element which is not observable among any of the interviewees, no matter which generation they belong to. None are fascinated by the German past and the Germanness of the town; none fully consciously accept the German heritage of the town as one's one, as is the case in Wrocław, Gdańsk or in the Mazury region,[12] where intellectuals have discovered the German cultural heritage and have quite successfully integrated it into their local identity. There are several possible explanations for the lack of this process, so common in other parts of the 'Regained Lands'. The first is the geographical position of the town. Since its founding in the middle of the nineteenth century, Krzyż has been located in a borderland: at first on the border of the German region, and then on the border with the Polish state, and finally on the border of the Polish voivodeships. This made its identity and character quite fluid and receptive to change. The existing literature describes such places as easier to 'Polonize' after the war than places of uniform, decidedly German character. Another reason is the lack of German cultural artefacts of special value which could serve as the basis for such a fascination. Krzyż is a relatively young town (founded in the mid-nineteenth century), and with the exception of two churches, there are no significant architectural monuments, nor were any famous Germans born in Krzyż. In a word, the Germanness of the town was quite easy to forget. Moreover, it seems that there is no influential group of people who would be interested in remembering and discovering Germanness there. In the aforementioned regions, where local Poles cultivate German cultural heritage, this process was started namely by the intelligentsia. In Krzyż local historians, teachers and cultural activists are fully aware of the town's German past, but do not see any special value in it.

---

11   Fałkowski, Mateusz: Razem w Unii. Niemcy w oczach Polaków 2000–2005, Warsaw: Instytut Spraw Publicznych, 2006.
12   Łukowski, Wojciech: Społeczne tworzenie ojczyzn. Studium tożsamości mieszkańców Mazur, Warsaw: Wydawnictwo Naukowe Scholar, 2002.

I would say that the general attitude of my interviewees to the German material culture can be defined as neutral. Just after the war, processes parallel to those happening in other areas of the 'Regained Lands' took place in Krzyż: monuments were destroyed, brick buildings were plastered, the interiors of Protestant churches were taken down and wooden verandas were added to the German stone or brick farms.[13] However, it seems that even then this process, if one is not talking about official propaganda but about people's opinions and feelings, was not characterized by hatred towards a space which was German, but rather by a desire to make the space more Polish and familiar. The fact that German buildings were not destroyed, as in other places, but only remodelled, converted to a form which was acceptable to the new inhabitants, serves as evidence for this hypothesis. The best example is the German cemetery in Krzyż. While in many other places German cemeteries were barbarously destroyed, in Krzyż the cemetery was just abandoned as a harmless and unnecessary place. No longer cared for, it fell into ruin and was partially destroyed at the end of nineties – again, not because it was German, but because more room was needed for the neighbouring Polish cemetery. When asked about this event today, interviewees reacted rather indifferently.

9.4. Conclusions

Returning to the questions asked in the introduction, I would say that a new community has been successfully constructed in Krzyż. Of course, it is an absolutely different community for the different generations. For the oldest interviewees, it is a community of coercion; they belong to this community because of the outcome of the war,[14] which was beyond their control. Had it not been for the war, they never would have come to Krzyż voluntarily. This circumstance greatly influenced their attitudes to the new place of settlement and caused problems in adaptation, which in the case of some repatriates still have meaning. For the younger generation, belonging to the community is obvious because they were born in Krzyż.

The new community is based mainly on rootedness in space, not in time. People feel truly attached to the place where they live, but do not have any special bonds linking them to the town's past. While the oldest interviewees were silently ignoring the past, the younger are less aware or even entirely unaware of it. At the same time, certain processes of constructing an imaginary relationship with a Polish past for the

---

13 Czarnuch, Zbigniew: Oswajanie krajobrazu. Polscy osadnicy w dorzeczu dolnej Warty, in: Mazur, Z. (ed.): Wokół niemieckiego dziedzictwa kulturowego na Ziemiach Północnych i Zachodnich, Poznań: Instytut Zachodni, 1997, pp. 169–190.

14 For a definition of 'trajectory' by F. Schütze, see: Riemann, Gerhard / Schütze, Fritz: 'Trajektoria' jako podstawowa koncepcja teoretyczna w analizach cierpienia i bezładnych procesów społecznych, in: Kultura i Społeczeństwo, 1992 (Vol. 36), No. 2, pp. 89–111.

region are evident. The younger generation derives their knowledge about local history from official sources more than from family transmission, which in the case of the middle generation resulted in some prejudices against the Germans.

General attitudes toward Germans, those remembered by the oldest interviewees from the war times and those currently visiting Krzyż, can be described as positive. The oldest generation was hardly influenced by the official anti-German propaganda as the basis for their opinion was their predominantly positive personal contact with the German population. Moreover, their attitude towards Germans as former householders of the town is characterized more by sympathy than by fear or distrust. The youngest generation perceives Germans mostly as normal tourists, economical partners etc., and not as the former owners of their homes.

Thus, research has shown without a doubt that history and the past matter, but less and less with each generation. Whether this is positive or negative we will see in the near future.

Part III. Civil Society and Globalization Pressures

Marlene Spoerri

10. Democratic Parties with Undemocratic Practices. Examining Foreign Assistance to Political Parties in Serbia

10.1. Introduction

Political parties have long been regarded as a staple of pluralist politics without which modern democracy is virtually inconceivable.[1] Nevertheless, while the importance of political parties to modern-day democracy is widely acknowledged, the utility of internal party democracy remains bitterly contested.[2] Where scholars such as Susan Scarrow maintain that it augments the participatory dimensions of representative democracy, others including Giovanni Sartori argue that internal party democracy is ultimately undesirable. Despite this controversy, Western governments have made support for intra-party democracy a core component of foreign assistance to political parties in new democracies. This chapter examines the effectiveness of such assistance in one new democracy, that of Serbia.

As shall be demonstrated, Serbia's political parties suffer from democratic deficits that are emblematic of post-communist parties. They are often dominated by charismatic leaders who take little note of the rank-and-file, are largely intolerant of internal dissent and boast decision-making processes which lack transparency. By almost any measure, they provide further credence to Robert Michels's iron law of oligarchy.[3] However, these very same parties have been the recipients of considerable foreign assistance aimed at bolstering their democratic credentials. For over a decade, their members sat through lectures and training courses aimed at democratizing their organizational practices. In some cases, they even accepted material assistance. But are Serbia's political parties today more internally democratic as a result? Or do persistent failings suggest that such aid is better directed elsewhere? As shall be shown, clear instances of success are few and far between. In many respects, Serbia's parties are no more democratic today – a full decade after the onset of foreign assistance – than they were some two decades ago.

To substantiate these claims, the following pages proceed by offering an overview of the foreign assistance effort to political parties in Serbia. This is followed with

---

1   See for example: van Biezen, Ingrid: How Political Parties Shape Democracy, Center for the Study of Democracy, Paper 04/16, 2004.
2   The terms 'internal party democracy' and 'intra-party democracy' are used interchangeably throughout this contribution.
3   According to which all organizations, parties included, are prone to oligarchic tendencies. Michels, Robert: Political Parties. A Sociological Study of the Oligarchical Tendencies of Modern Democracy, New York/NY: The Free Press, 1962.

an in-depth analysis of how party structures have evolved since the onset of multi-party politics in 1990. The chapter concludes with a general assessment of the utility of foreign assistance. First, however, the text begins by examining the theory underpinning intra-party democracy.

10.2. Intra-party Democracy

Studies on intra-party democracy explore how political parties govern themselves. This includes how parties reach the decisions they make, what steps they take to ensure that those decisions are in tune with the will of their membership, and the lengths to which they go to protect the rights of members who do not share the majority opinion. More specifically, intra-party democracy, also known as internal party democracy, refers to those mechanisms that make parties' governance processes more inclusive and more representative of the party membership in its entirety.[4]

Studies of intra-party democracy focus on one or more of the following three dimensions of party organization: inclusiveness, referring to how extensive or representative the group of party decision-makers is; centralization, or how often decisions are made by only a single body; and institutionalization, pertaining to how formalized the procedures of governance are. An internally democratic party is likely to boast governance methods which are inclusive, at least partially though not necessarily wholly decentralized, and institutionalized. By contrast, parties that suffer democratic deficiencies tend towards exclusivity (with a limited, unrepresentative set of party members holding decision-making powers), go to extremes in either centralization or decentralization (to such a degree that the final outcome does not reflect the will of the general party membership), and/or tend to be poorly institutionalized (although the opposite may also be true, as rules of exclusivity may be firmly in place).

Amidst their efforts to spread democracy abroad, governments in North America and Western Europe support projects that aim to bolster parties' democratic attributes. This means, among other things, helping the governance processes of political parties in new democracies become more inclusive, less centralized and further institutionalized. Efforts targeting intra-party democracy form just one instrument of what is a larger tool kit known as political party assistance (henceforth, PPA). PPA, in turn, is one of a handful of instruments falling under the domain of democracy aid. Like diplomacy, economic incentives, and more controversially, military intervention, democracy aid forms an integral part of the burgeoning field of democracy promotion.

Yet although PPA forms but a single – and by no means, the most prominent – facet of democracy assistance, bolstering intra-party democracy is arguably 'the single

---

4   Scarrow, Susan: Political Parties and Democracy in Theoretical and Practical Perspectives. Implementing Intra-Party Democracy, National Democracy Institute for International Affairs, 2005, p. 6.

most common objective party aid groups talk about when they discuss their work'[5]. Indeed, there seems to be wide consensus amongst donors that intra-party democracy is both a desirable and feasible objective.

This consensus is surprising in light of the intense controversy that surrounds intra-party democracy in the academic world. Critiques of intra-party democracy are so numerous, in fact, that three different variants can be distinguished: the argument that it is impossible to achieve, the belief that it is undesirable and the conviction that it is ultimately harmful.[6] However, donors appear to take no heed of such arguments. They are convinced that the benefits of intra-party democracy extend not only to parties themselves but also to the larger democratic process. Their means of defence is thus at once both normative and instrumental. With regards to the former, assisters argue that in drawing their members into the folds of decision making, the distance between the elector and the elected is narrowed, and the democratic process thereby enhanced.[7] But they also believe that intra-party democracy can potentially provide political parties a competitive edge. Susan Scarrow writes that

> ...parties using internally democratic procedures are likely to select more capable and appealing leaders, to have more responsive policies, and, as a result, to enjoy greater electoral success.[8]

It is for these reasons that foreign governments support efforts to democratize parties' governance processes.

There is surprisingly little variation with respect to the methods by which intra-party democracy is supported. Thus party aid providers will seek to: 1) lecture party leaders on the benefits of intra-party democracy; 2) provide expertise on the subject; 3) train rank-and-file members on internal party communication; 4) train top party brass on how to implement and interpret intra-party opinion polls; 5) support events (including party congresses, conferences, etc.) during which the subject of intra-party democracy may be debated by party members, and 6) have party representatives from other new democracies share their own party's successes. The following section examines how these tools have been employed in Serbia.

---

5   Carothers, Thomas: Confronting the Weakest Link. Aiding Political Parties in New Democracies, Washington D. C.: Carnegie Endowment for International Peace, 2006, p. 95.
6   To this first group belong Robert Michels and Petr Ostrogorski. The second group includes Giovanni Sartori and Elmer E. Schattschneider. Maurice Duverger and John May belong, among others, to the third group.
7   Magolowondo, Augustine Titani: Internal Party Democracy. The State of Affairs and the Road Ahead, Netherlands Institute of Multiparty Politics, 2007, p. 2.
8   Scarrow, Susan: Political Parties and Democracy in Theoretical and Practical Perspectives. Implementing Intra-Party Democracy, National Democracy Institute for International Affairs, 2005, p. 3.

10.3. Political Party Assistance in Serbia

Multiple actors are engaged in the provision of external support to political parties in Serbia. Certainly the highest profile actors, as well as those with the greatest budgets at their disposal, are the American party institutes: the International Republican Institute (IRI) and the National Democratic Institute of International Affairs (NDI). Somewhat less well endowed bodies are the five German foundations – the *Stiftungen* – of which the Friedrich Ebert Stiftung (FES) and Konrad Adenauer Stiftung (KAS) are the most active in the field of party work.[9] In addition, the UK's Westminster Foundation for Democracy provides support to political parties in Serbia, as do – on a far smaller scale – numerous sister parties throughout Western Europe.

In most instances, donors have been working in Serbia for just over a decade, having set up shop in the immediate aftermath of the Zajedno demonstrations. For four months, from November 1996 to February 1997, Serbia's democratic opposition launched daily protests against the Milosevic regime. It was the magnitude and longevity of these demonstrations that placed Serbia on the radar of the world's promoters of democracy. Convinced that a democratic dawn was upon them, donors set their sights on Serbia's democratic parties.

The earliest efforts concentrated on the larger members of Serbia's democratic opposition, including the Serbian Renewal Movement (SPO) and the Democratic Party (DS), but were soon expanded to include smaller parties such as the Democratic Party of Serbia (DSS). In the aftermath of regime change, aid providers would add to that list some of Serbia's youngest parties, among them the G17 Plus and the Liberal Democratic Party (LDP). All the while, however, pro-establishment parties like the Serbian Radical Party and the Socialist Party of Serbia were excluded from foreign support with the justification that they harboured anti-democratic sentiments.[10] As such, only the aforementioned five parties – the DS, DSS, G17 Plus, LDP, and SPO – will be the focus of this chapter.

The initial wave of foreign assistance was little more than of a token of what was to come. In some cases (the German *Stiftungen* for example), donors relied exclusively on one or two local operatives working from their homes. In others (the IRI and NDI), donors hired foreign resident directors who were charged with opening offices and scouting out potential partners. The first projects donors supported were similarly modest. Having come on the heels of oppositional victories in former Milosevic-strongholds like Kragujevac, Nis, Cacak and Novi Sad, aid providers began by focusing

---

9   Of the six German Stiftungen, only the Rosa Luxemburg Stiftung is not active in Serbia.
10   Throughout my interview with party aid providers, the SRS and SPS were labelled 'anti-demo-cratic'. Western donors have largely held off from working with such parties. See for example: USAID Political Party Assistance Policy, Washington D. C.: United States Agency for International Development, 2003.

on the mechanics of party organization. Given that most parties in Serbia either lacked local branches and/or were terribly under-resourced outside of Belgrade, most of the first training courses were simple capacity-building measures based on the transfer of basic skills. According to Ellen Yount, IRI's first resident director in Serbia,

> [t]he purpose of aid funding [at this period] was to bring more transparency to the political process. Milosevic had an overwhelming advantage in terms of resources, monopoly of media, etc. We helped parties to try to understand the tools and techniques they needed to stay on a level playing field.[11]

As time passed, donors branched out into further areas, shifting from activities that were solely focused on local party offices to national headquarters.

By 1999, the war in Kosovo had broken out and the removal of Milosevic topped the international agenda. Levels of foreign assistance to Serbia's democratic opposition rose considerably during this period.[12] Attention shifted to those efforts that donors' believed would most rapidly result in regime change. Perhaps understandably, intra-party democracy was not amongst these efforts. Only after Milosevic was ousted in October 2000 did intra-party democracy become a chief concern for foreign donors. Indeed, aid provider reports and promotional literature continue to list intra-party democracy as one of just a handful of critical goals to be accomplished in Serbia. To this end, Serbia's parties have been the target of a transatlantic effort to strengthen internal democratic practices. Thus, the IRI has helped parties conduct internal public opinion polls so that the will of the membership might be clearly assessed. The German *Stiftungen* have provided support for party conferences in which internal party democracy was a subject of discussion. At the same time, the NDI, which arguably has placed the greatest emphasis on intra-party democracy, has provided training and material support for intranet-based communication systems and has also offered expertise on how to implement more inclusive selection methods, particularly those based on a US-like primary system.

The following pages assess the effects of such efforts by examining the range of choices Serbia's political parties have made with respect to intra-party democracy. In so doing, this chapter relies not only on party statutes, but also on interviews with party members and domestic media reports, both of which help to elucidate the state of intra-party democracy in practice.

---

11   Interview with Ellen Yount in Washington D. C., 14 April 2008.
12   See for example: Carothers, Thomas: Ousting Foreign Strongmen. Lessons Learned from Serbia, Carnegie Endowment for International Peace, Policy Brief, 2001 (Vol. 1), No. 5.

10.4. The Evolution of Intra-Party Democracy in Serbia

By general consensus, Serbia's parties leave much to be desired when it comes to internal democracy.[13] Like most parties in post-communist Europe, they are dominated by strong leaders, intolerant of internal dissent and poorly institutionalized.[14] Certainly, when parties were first formed in the early 1990s their democratic deficits were abundant. Vesna Pesic, a former party president herself, explains it thus: the lack of intra-party democracy in Serbia

> [...] was understandable when the only goal was bringing down the Milosevic regime. It was not necessary to develop wider forms of internal democracy [...].[15]

But are there indications that Serbia's parties are gradually becoming more democratic? Is there reason to believe that foreign assistance is working in this regard? To answer these questions, this section examines the evolution of four key aspects of intra-party organization: the prerogatives assigned to party presidents, the methods of leader election, the means of candidate selection and the rules regarding internal dissent.

10.5. Presidential Prerogatives

Historically, Serbia's party presidents have played a central role in their parties' decision-making processes. In most cases, they oversaw the founding of their parties. In some instances, party presidents have even come to define them.[16] Oddly, however, considering their infamous reputations in the 1990s, Serbia's party presidents have actually grown more, rather than less, powerful with the passing of time. Despite the calls from those giving assistance for greater inclusivity in the decision-making process, the growing concentration of power in party leaders' hands suggests that parties have steadily become more exclusive and less democratic as a result.

Serbia's first party statutes awarded surprisingly limited powers to the top party brass. The DS statute of 1990, for example, claimed its president's sole prerogative was that of calling the main board into session.[17] The powers of the DSS president were portrayed as similarly meagre in the party's first statute issued in 1992. Over the course of the following decade, however, party statutes awarded an ever greater array of powers to the position of the party president. Thus, by 1998, the DSS president formally

---

13   See for example: Goati, Vladimir: Partijske borbe u Srbiji u postoktobarskom razdoblju, Belgrade: Friedrich Ebert Stiftung, 2006.
14   This is confirmed in the work of Ingrid van Biezen, Petr Kopecky, and Paul G. Lewis, among others.
15   Pesic, Vesna: (De)Blokiranje tranzicije i unutarstranacka demokratija, in: Lutovac, Zoran (ed.): Demokratija u Politickim Strankama Srbije, Belgrade: Friedrich Ebert Stiftung, 2006, p. 23.
16   This is certainly the case for the SPO and DSS, neither of which has experienced a change in leadership.
17   DS Statute 1990, Art. 14.

had the right to coordinate party work, to propose candidates for the executive board and vice presidents, as well as to compose an electoral list of MPs. By 2001, he or she was also awarded the power to initiate dismissal procedures for the party presidium, council and electoral board. Today, presidents' powers are even more impressive.

Thus, amongst other prerogatives, the LDP president can: lead the work of the presidium; propose candidates for the presidium, party secretary and presidium secretary; propose candidates for main party functionaries on the national level; nominate the party spokesperson, and recommend an unlimited number of members to be co-opted to the main board.[18] The G17 Plus party president is somewhat weaker, but also has the right to propose a large number – up to sixty – permanent members on the main board.[19] For the DSS, the prerogatives of the president stretch even further: he or she is charged with nominating all the members of the presidium (including all the party's vice presidents), up to twenty-four members of the main board, three members of the party's monitoring board, as well as all members of the party's disciplinary commission.[20] According to the DS's latest statute, the party president may select candidates for deputy president, vice president, members of the presidium, president of the executive board, secretary and director of the party, secretary of the presidium and members of the political council.[21]

The increasing institutionalization of power in the hands of party leaders has occurred progressively and shows little sign of abating. While it does not necessarily indicate that party presidents have grown more powerful *per se* (party statutes having been poorly elaborated in the 1990s), it certainly indicates that PPA has done little to stem the tide of top-down party politics.

10.6. Leader Election

Given their considerable powers, the means by which party leaders are elected is of considerable importance. For advocates of intra-party democracy, aid providers included, it is arguably the most important aspect of a party's organizational life. In Serbia, the process of selecting leaders has historically been and in most cases remains a tightly controlled affair. As has been the case for almost two decades, party statutes dictate that leaders are elected at party congresses, a body which includes hundreds or, in some cases, thousands of members. Throughout the 1990s, electoral processes were largely uncompetitive and under-institutionalized. The DSS's president, for example, ran unopposed for the entire decade. Moreover, party statutes were silent with regards to the details of the electoral process. It was unclear, for example, how

18   LDP Statute 2007, Art. 24.
19   G17 Plus State 2006, Art. 31.
20   DSS Statute 2007, Art. 22, Art. 16, Art. 86, Art. 15.
21   DS Statute 2006, Art. 39.

potential competitors might be nominated. If we measure levels of leadership turnover, we see that of the three parties under review which were operational in the period between 1990 and 1997 (DS, DSS, and SPO), just one experienced a change in leadership: the DS.

There is no systemic evidence that internal electoral processes have become any less problematic since the onset of PPA. While electoral processes have certainly been further elucidated in party documents,[22] these rules and regulations are rarely upheld in practice. A prime example is the rule of the secret ballot. In 2004, the DS's congress caused considerable stir when the president of the DS's Electoral Committee alleged that prior to their submission the ballots of assembly delegates from local municipalities were screened by municipal presidents.[23] Two years later suspicions were further aroused when in the days preceding the assembly meeting documents were uncovered revealing the precise outcome of the congress' decisions. Although the DS affair was certainly the highest profile case of fraud, there is little reason to suspect that it occurred in isolation.

Arguably, however, some good did come of the DS's debacles. In 2006, the DS unveiled a dramatic step towards greater intra-party democracy: the introduction of the primary system. Beginning in 2010, DS presidents will be elected by *all* party members through a secret ballot system. This represents a major departure from standard practice and could, quite possibly, set a precedent for the rest of Serbia's parties to follow.

Unfortunately, the DS's decision is the exception, not the rule. Electoral processes are largely closed affairs and have improved little with respect to competition. Indeed, since the onset of assistance, just two of the five parties reviewed here have experienced a change in leadership: the DS and G17 Plus. In the case of the DS, it was in fact only the assassination of the party leader which prompted the transition. Such evidence suggests that, on the whole, we can only speak of limited improvement in electoral practices.

10.7. Candidate Selection

Candidate selection is also important for proponents of intra-party democracy. In any representative democracy, one of political parties' most important functions is that of recruiting individuals (i.e. candidates) who will run for office in their name.[24] Over

---

22 Party documents currently provide greater insight into nomination procedures, for example.
23 Gligorijevic, Jovana: Skupstina Demokratske Stranke. Kontrolisani Glasovi, in: Vreme, No. 790, 23 February 2006, http://www.vreme.com/cms/view.php?id=444128. This phenomenon was also confirmed during my interviews with former DS members.
24 See for example: van Biezen, Ingrid: How Political Parties Shape Democracy, Center for the Study of Democracy, Paper 04/16, 2004.

the course of the past two decades, the selection of candidates has been and indeed remains an inordinately centralized and exclusive procedure. Unlike the election of candidates, there is virtually no indication that such processes have become any more democratic since the onset of PPA.

In the 1990s, party statutes maintained that party presidents and presidencies played the central role in candidate selection by determining the potential pool of party MPs. It was thus this small party elite (in some cases, an individual) which composed the list of MPs. Although it was ultimately up to the main board to approve that list, they often did so with little deliberation.

This process remains virtually identical today, with the only exception being that the statutes of the DS and DSS now explicitly state that party presidents should take the wishes of municipal boards into consideration.

10.8. Tolerance of Internal Dissent

One of the basic principles of intra-party democracy concerns the right of party members to voice their opinions openly and without fear of reprisal. Ideally, it also means that members have the right to act or organize on the basis of those opinions, and even to form factions if they so desire. As shall be shown, the evolution of party tolerance in Serbia is somewhat contradictory in this respect.

The parties' inability to accommodate internal dissent was legendary throughout the 1990s. Then, as today, no party permitted internal factions; nor did they in practice allow members to organize on the basis of such differences. One product of their intolerance was a spin-off effect, whereby minority groups would splinter off to form their own rival organizations. During this period, the DS alone was directly responsible for having spawned three separate parties.[25] These parties, in turn, became a source of further off-shoots. Thus, in 1997 disgruntled DSS members went on to form the Christian Democratic Party of Serbia. In 1995, members were put off by Vuk Draskovic's authoritarian tendencies and left the SPO to form the Assembly National Party. In the past few years, the number of parties formed as offshoots has dropped considerably. The most recent examples are the creation of the LDP (an offshoot of the DS) and the formation of the Serbian Democratic Renewal Movement (formerly of the SPO). This would seem to indicate that parties have become more accommodating to competing perspectives.

However, there is equally powerful evidence that political parties have become even more intolerant, a prime example of which is Serbia's new constitution which effectively places MPs' mandates at their parties' disposal.[26] In contrast to the 1990s,

---

25 These were: the DSS, the Serbian Liberal Party, and Democratic Center.
26 Constitution of the Republic of Serbia, 2006, Art. 102, http://www.parlament.sr.gov.yu/content/eng/akta/ustav/ustav_ceo.asp

Serbia's parties thus currently have the right to revoke their MPs' mandates at any time and place someone of their own choosing. In practical terms, this means that MPs are no longer free to vote as their conscience dictates but must abide by the party line. This unprecedented ruling effectively represents the further institutionalization of the party's power over individual party members. It is in fact a major step *away* from the further democratization of Serbia's political parties.

10.9. Conclusion. A Slim Record of Achievement?

The story sketched above is troubling for many reasons. Political apathy runs high throughout Serbia and a lack of intra-party democracy does little to deter it. My own interviews with current and former party members exposed significant disillusionment with the state of internal party politics. Hence the commonness of statements like 'Ceda is an autocrat'[27] or 'we are not yet ready for internal party democracy.'[28] Few party members admitted to being part of the decision-making process. Many expressed frustration at their own inability to bring about change and the top-down manner in which decisions were made. As a consequence, quite a few of those with whom I spoke had either abandoned their positions within their parties or opted to withdraw from party life at the time of writing. The parties' habit of ostracizing their most competent members only hampers the larger political process and arguably threatens the longevity of democracy in Serbia.

It is for reasons such as these that donors have sought to support the democratization of Serbia's political parties. In many respects, it seems they have failed. Apart from a few scattered victories (of which the DS's future use of the primary voting system ranks highest), they can point to few overarching successes. This is a verdict all too familiar for practitioners on the ground, but one which donors have yet to accept. In my discussions with party trainers working in Serbia, many expressed frustration with the mission they had been given. In the words of one practitioner, 'internal democracy is not realistic. I can't afford, as a professional, to have some set goals that are not achievable.'[29] According to another – a former resident director of NDI – in fact, 'internal party democracy means nothing.'[30] But if practitioners themselves are so sceptical, why do they bother? Quite simply, because intra-party democracy sells – at least amongst the assistance community. Regardless of the ample criticisms which have been lodged against the endeavour, donors are convinced of its normative value and are willing to devote resources accordingly.

---

27 Ceda refers to the name of LDP's president, Cedomir Jovanovic. Interview with LDP party member, Belgrade, 26 June 2007.
28 Interview with a DSS party member, Strasbourg, 3 July 2007.
29 Interview with a former NDI party trainer, Belgrade, 9 March 2007.
30 Interview with a former NDI resident director, 20 April 2007, location undisclosed.

The issue here is not that donors have identified intra-party democracy as desirable. The problem lies in their assumption that they have the means to bring it about. However, there is scant evidence that democracy promoters can succeed in this regards.[31] Although they can certainly lead by example, there is little reason to suspect that internal party democracy can be fostered by actors outside the political process itself. This does not imply that donors give up the endeavour entirely, but that they are more modest in their goals and more explicit with regards to what is feasible. Helping parties change themselves might very well require the lowering of donors' expectations.

---

31   See for example: Kumar, Krishna: Reflections on International Political Party Assistance, in: Democratization, 2005 (Vol. 12), No. 4, pp. 505–527.

Emira Ibrahimpasic

11. Agency Through Struggle. Muslim Women's Identities in Secular Bosnia-Herzegovina

11.1. Introduction

This contribution is the result of a ten-month research project in Sarajevo, Bosnia, and Herzegovina funded by an International Research and Exchange Program Individual Advanced Research Opportunities Grant. Using ethnographic methods of participant observation, one-on-one interviews, personal stories, focus groups, open-ended lengthy surveys of religiosity, and network studies, I explored some of the ways in which Muslim women in Bosnia and Herzegovina exert agency and reject the characterization of victimhood so often placed upon them by foreign researchers and scholars. This research also examines how religious belief and practice help women attain status and prestige within a secular state. The main objective of this project was to investigate how Islam helps women to deal with the daily challenges brought on by the political and economic problems commonly found in a post-war environment. Most importantly, this project explores acts of power and rebellion achieved through religious belief and practice.

There are two ways in which the popular media, both in Bosnia and beyond, has come to portray Muslim women. One image revolves around the 'rural and/or religious Bosniak woman wearing a head scarf, as a symbol of (Bosniak) national suffering or identity.'[1] The other is that of an empowered, educated, emancipated woman who has shed the restrictive bounds of Islam and has successfully been integrated into European society and culture. These two 'types' are diametrically opposed: One represents tradition while the other embodies modernization.

The two images rarely meet, and the ideologies that guide both characterizations are perceived to be so at odds with each other that the possibility of a third kind of Muslim woman is rarely acknowledged or discussed. Moreover, these types of representations further enhance the historical frictions between East and West.

In this chapter I challenge the negative images of religious Muslim women and explore the significance of the small, faith-based networks organized by young women in Sarajevo, who are often mistakenly characterized as uneducated, poor and rural. In addition, I explore ways in which small, faith-based networks are both reinforc-

---

1   Helms, Elissa: Gendered Visions of the Bosnian Future. Women's Activism and Representation in Post-war Bosnia-Herzegovina, Dissertation, University of Pittsburgh, 2003, p. 199.

ing 'Islamic gender roles'[2] and helping to re-establish a new gender order rooted in religious traditions and practice. Finally, I show how these networks help women exert agency in a system that often silences their voices and empower themselves in a society that continuously contests their faith.

11.2. Networks

As an institution, religion was allowed to exist in socialist Yugoslavia, but it was suppressed. Public displays of religious belief and practice, such as wearing the veil and frequenting religious institutions, were seen as expressions of nationalism, and were therefore deemed as anti-state behaviour.[3] Apprehension about publicly displaying belief and practice, in addition to the fear of ethnic cleansing, has permeated the social consciousness of Bosnia's Muslims. Consequently, many devout women are reluctant to display, speak about, or discuss religion publicly. One countermeasure to this uneasy climate has been the creation of small, faith-based networks.

Within the context of my research project, I define faith-based networks as possessing the following characteristics: a) six to fifteen members; b) common religious belief and practice; c) common interests as they relate to furthering religious knowledge; d) social and moral support for all members; and finally, f) personal connection to at least one member of the group in order to gain entry initially. Additionally, small, faith-based groups serve a variety of purposes for each individual member. In this chapter I identify four main functions, including: 1) providing support to members; 2) giving women a space where they can discuss issues they encounter in their everyday lives; 3) helping women create a moral community rooted in religious doctrine; and finally, 4) allowing women to reach out and recruit other members who share their beliefs, practices and experiences. Finally, in forming these crucial friendships, women choose to favour religious orientation over other character traits.

Small, faith-based networks play an important role in helping women create ties that extend beyond the private sphere. In Yugoslavia, women were active participants in the workforce and held minor political positions; however, this did not trans-

---

2   Since Islam is not a monolith, but rather a collection of various meanings, interpretations and practices, I define 'Islamic gender roles' in the context of Bosnia's traditional Islamic practices concerning women. Bosnian Muslim women, as descendants of Ottomans, practice a Sunni form of Islam. This legacy is characterized by strict gender segregation, relegation of women to the private sphere, and a lack of public (and therefore political) activity. Cf.: Mernissi, Fatima: The Veil and the Male Elite. A Feminist Interpretation of Women's Rights in Islam, New York/NY: Basic Books, 1991; Wadud, Amina: Inside the gender Jihad. Women's reform in Islam, Oxford: Oneworld Publications, 2006.

3   Doubt, Keith: Islam and Bosnia. Conflict resolution and foreign policy in multi-ethnic societies, in: Sociology of Religion, 2005 (Vol. 66), No. 1, pp. 92–93.

late into egalitarian gender relations.[4] Entry into the public sphere, along with explicit and public displays of religious belief and practice, has been difficult since the end of the war. Therefore, the creation of small, faith-based networks has become an essential and necessary part of these women's lives.

11.3. Context

In order to conduct my research, I became active in a faith-based NGO and also joined a strong network of women unconnected to it. Women-centred networks are common in Bosnia, especially among Muslim women. Many of my informants argue that this is most likely a result of Ottoman traditions and the strict gender roles instituted by Islam, which was the chosen faith of the Ottomans. In the Holy Qur'an surrah (chapter) 24, verse 31, it is forbidden for men and women to see each other unless they are related or married. Interpretations of this chapter have led to the creation of separate spaces for men and women, with women and men occupying the private and public spheres of social life, respectively.[5] Accordingly, women and men have created networks primarily made up of members of their own sex.[6] Given that Muslim, and Christian, women in Bosnia were accorded fairly equal access to the public sphere during the past seventy years, I found it puzzling to see so many religious women struggling with access to the public sphere. In the aftermath of the civil war, women were relegated to the domestic sphere in greater numbers than before. This relegation was even truer for Muslim women due to the more orthodox forms of Islam imported from Arab countries, which assign stricter gender roles. As a result, I argue that strong women's networks are not new and are a direct result of these historical influences.

During my research I became a part of one such group whose members were primarily unmarried, young, urban women who described themselves as 'vjernice', or 'believers'. 'Vjernica' refers to a woman who observes Islamic belief and practice. While the term 'vjernica' is self-ascribed, it generally implies several basic elements: 1) belief in Allah as the only God and creator of all things; 2) observance of some of the main

---

4   Funk, Nanette / Mueller, Magda: Gender politics and post-communism. Reflections from Eastern Europe and the former Soviet Union, New York/NY: Routledge, 1993; Hunt, Swanee: Muslim women in the Bosnian crucible, in: Sex Roles, 2004 (Vol. 5) No. 5–6, pp. 301–317; Morokvasic, Mirjana (ed.): Being a Woman in Yugoslavia. Past, Present and Institutional Equality, London, New York/NY: Zed Books, 1986.

5   Abu-Lughod, Lila: Writing Women's Worlds. Bedouin Stories, Berkeley/CA: University of California Press, 1993; Eickelman, Christine: Women and Community in Oman, New York/NY: New York University Press, 1984.

6   Abu-Lughod, Lila: Writing Women's Worlds. Bedouin Stories, Berkeley/CA: University of California Press, 1993; Eickelman, Christine: Women and Community in Oman, New York/NY: New York University Press, 1984; Fernea, Elizabeth Warnock: Guests of the Sheik, London: Hale, 1968; Mernissi, Fatima: The Veil and the Male Elite. A Feminist Interpretation of Women's Rights in Islam, New York/NY: Basic Books, 1991; Wikan, Unni: Behind the veil in Arabia. Women in Oman, Chicago/IL: University of Chicago Press, 1991.

Islamic holidays, including Ramadan and Eid Mubarak; and 3) declaration of oneself as a Muslim. For the women in my group, the term 'vjernica' included four additional rules: a) prayer five times a day; b) no alcohol consumption; c) no extramarital sex; and d) observance of the majority of laws prescribed by the Qur'an and Haddith[7]. While I cannot be sure that all group members followed all of these rules, my observations suggest that they did. Group meetings focused on discussion of faith, belief and practice, and generally included a group prayer at a nearby mosque or attendance of a religious-oriented event.

11.4. Case Studies

I became part of this informal faith-based network through my connections at Nahla, a faith-based educational organization for women. At Nahla, I attended the School of Islam and participated in a systematic education programme that enhanced my knowledge of Islamic belief, practice and life. Once I had acquired the connections, skills and knowledge taught at the school, I was able to fully participate in conversations in any Islamic-centred setting about religious belief and practice. Subsequently, I was able to be fully integrated into the group.

11.4.1.   Building a Cohesive Moral Group

Our faith-based network met only in places that it deemed 'moral' and where members felt that like-minded people would surround them. In this setting, religious discussions were considered appropriate. One night, thirteen young women between the ages of twenty-one and twenty-seven sat together in a large circle drinking coffee and tea. Some were veiled; others were not. They came from a variety of educational and socio-economic backgrounds and geographic locations. All of the women had come of age in post-Yugoslavia and at the time, all were single and/or engaged to be married.

One of my primary informants, Envera[8], revealed that she had been thinking of different ways for us to draw more young people towards faith. Although we had never before discussed this topic, the entire group became engaged in the conversation. Women suggested classes, meeting places, and innovative ways of mentoring youth.

Through suggestions, conversations, and critiques of mainstream society's lack of concern for youth, the young women found their voice. Belkisa, a 24-year-old recent Faculty of Law graduate, suggested that the tone of condescension with which religious people and adults in general addressed young people had to be changed.

---

7   Collection of reports on the actions and statements made by the Prophet Mohammed.
8   In this document, all of the informants' names are pseudonyms.

Envera agreed with this and added that because of the hierarchical nature of families, the majority of religious leaders (outside Bugari[9]) had a difficult time speaking to adults and even more so to teenagers. Ajla suggested that we focus on creating a safe space for teenagers where they could come and talk about problems without feeling judged. Envera agreed, underscoring the need for young people to be listened to, rather than punished and judged.

The conversation was engaging, and the women said they felt comfortable expressing their opinions in a nonjudgmental environment. Their emphasis on the ability to speak their minds during the conversation was in fact a symptom of their position in Bosnian society. Whether or not they wore a headscarf (which only a few did) as a visual symbol of their faith and dedication to Islam, most of the women in the group felt as if their faith was contested on a daily basis. The group allowed the women to express opinions deeply rooted in religious dogma that were likely to be dismissed by people outside the group.

I asked Envera later what had prompted her to bring up the topic of bringing more young people into the fold of Islamic faith. She said her primary motivation was the lack of morality she witnessed every day. She also asserted that there were fewer and fewer young people who were religious, or who even knew anything about Islam. She therefore felt that it was important to create a network in which young people felt safe and not judged due to a lack of knowledge about religious faith and practice.

This type of discussion is only one example of the ways in which young women in Bosnia are expressing their identities not only as Muslims, but also as educated, caring and empowered women. In secular societies, religiosity is often seen as working against state formation; however, these young women are actively building community networks and institutions that serve important social roles within the state. Their efforts to organize forums to help others exemplify this type of personal agency. This particular interaction demonstrates all four goals of the group, especially in creating moral community and networking.

11.4.2. Marriage

Marriage was a common topic among group members. All of the women were single or engaged at the time, and the group provided a forum in which women could discuss intimate details and ask questions that were not addressed in religious texts. Concerning marriage, Belkisa said, 'Part of being a good Muslim woman involves being a good wife and mother'. According to the Qur'an, marriage, as a set of beliefs

---

9   Sulejman Bugari is a famous Bosnian imam who has become vastly popular among young people within the past decade. He is a hafiz (i.e. someone who has completely memorized the Qur'an) and an Islamic scholar who runs anti-drug campaigns, drug rehabilitation centres, and writes best-selling books on the themes of Islam, belief and practice.

and principles, is an indispensable part of Islam. Group members argued that the only way a woman could gain emancipation from society's 'over-sexualized' female body was through marriage. As these women understood it, marriage was an answer to the lack of respect for women, which they believe has been polluting society. Belkisa commented that 'Modern society sees women as bodies to be objectified, and there is no more respect for the important work women do', and expressed her dissatisfaction with what she deemed 'immoral dating practices including pre-marital sex'. Like many group members, Belkisa believed that pre-marital sex leads to the exploitation of women by men. Marriage, as a contract, was the only way in which a woman could protect her virginity and secure her future. Guarding their chastity was important to these women, not only because Islam deems pre-marital sex a sin, but also because sex was one of the primary ways in which 'men used women'. According to the members of the group, the only way to get respect from men, and to respect themselves, was to observe this abstinence rule in everyday life.

Understanding marriage as a protective union in a world that has been hyper-sexualized by the media and the forces of globalization is one of the ways that members of the group empowered themselves. These women saw sex as a risk, a bargain that left them without security. In their eyes, control of their sexuality was emancipation from a norm rooted in Western ideals. These women attempted to redefine the image of a modern Bosnian woman as educated, empowered and active in rebuilding a new Bosnian landscape while simultaneously remaining deeply rooted in Islam.

11.4.3. Allegories

Other meetings centred on the discussion of religious texts, including the Qur'an and the Haddith. In addition, we often discussed the Islam-related websites that many of the young women in the group monitored, as they pertained to proper Islamic belief and practice. On one occasion, a young woman in her mid-twenties, Jasmina, brought up a story she had recently read on a Bosnian-language website about a man in his twenties who had married an apparently pious Muslim woman after both had completed their education at the Faculty of Islamic Studies. However, during their first night together, the young man found out that his wife was not a virgin, but because he was in love, all was forgiven. Things seemed to be going well until he realized that while married to him, this pious and veiled woman was seen walking around town with other men. When the rumour of her infidelity was confirmed, the only option available for the man was divorce[10].

---

10   Divorce is common in Islamic tradition. Rules state that a man cannot divorce a woman unless she agrees, and he must be willing to pay out the sum agreed upon at the time of marriage.

Group meetings typically revolved around stories such as this one; every week a different topic was presented in the hopes of drawing out a lesson that could be applied in day-to-day life. The moral of the story above was that you can't judge a book by its cover: a person can look pious yet be deceitful. The young woman seemed religiously observant but in fact lacked moral judgment and did not adhere to a proper Islamic lifestyle, and she duped the young man. After relating the story, Jasmina was eager to hear the other women's reactions.

Envera, a 24-year-old architecture student who had starting wearing a veil just within the last year, responded by speaking of the shame that this woman's behaviour brought upon all other veiled women. Alija, a 23-year-old student of law, reacted to the tale by relating a similar story involving people she knew. The young women gasped as they listened to another story of betrayal involving what appeared to be a pious Muslim woman.

In addition to these stories, the members of the group also discussed their personal experiences. Envera recalled the negative reactions toward her since she had begun wearing the veil. While her reasons for veiling were strictly 'to please Allah', she was not entirely impervious to the influence of her family, friends and colleagues. Envera's decision was deeply personal, and it took years to make. Indeed, she had a hard time coming to terms with the struggles she would have to face for the rest of her life as an overtly observant Muslim. However, she said that her decision to veil, despite the obvious day-to-day discrimination she would encounter, was empowering. It involved a struggle that required her to literally wear her choice on her body, a decision that had resulted in scorn, insults and sometimes violence for those who had made the choice before her.

Envera used her small group as a support system, and her decision to veil was reinforced. She is the exact opposite of the image of the oppressed, disempowered, voiceless practicing Muslim woman that the popular Western media has propagated. She is educated, widely connected, and one of the primary organizers of this particular faith-based group. Most importantly, as a veiled woman, she is well aware that her appearance and public representation of Islam is unpopular. Envera has made her faith and practice, which are deeply personal, public and political. This kind of statement, used since the dawn of the feminist movement in the West, has been successfully transplanted and employed by women like Envera.

This particular discussion demonstrates how small, faith-based networks have served to achieve the group's important goal of providing women with a community whose foundation is shared beliefs and ideology. In addition, the telling and retelling of stories they had heard or read was an important part of building a community and provided a moral compass for all members. This new community was particularly important because many of the women had a difficult time explaining their beliefs and practice to those closest to them, especially family members. Much scholarship has shown that storytelling and narratives are often used to explain life experiences. In addition, storytelling allows these young women to deal with problematic and unexpected situations in their daily lives.

11.5. Conclusion

This contribution is an attempt to illuminate the complexity of what it means to be a Muslim, and specifically a Muslim woman, in contemporary Bosnia. Exploring the ways in which young, self-described religious Muslim women construct and re-construct social networks is an important step to understanding the role of religion in women's lives.[11] My participant observation of a small, faith-based network suggests that young women form networks, sometimes more than one, as a way of carving out a space for themselves within a new social order. The war of independence from Yugoslavia (1992–1995) severely disrupted kin- and community-based networks, and many people have had a very difficult time reconstituting such networks in the post-war social environment. Women, including the members of 'my' group, cannot always turn to their nuclear families or other kin-based networks for community and are therefore forced to look for alternative spaces for themselves in the new Bosnia. The creation of small, faith-based groups is an extension of the complex set of networks that guide and define Bosnia's social, economic and political spheres.

In post-war Bosnia, young religious women are reconstituting networks that are rooted in common ideology and Islamic beliefs. These networks provide a safe haven and a support system where women can create and exercise identities that they feel might not be accepted or understood by those outside the group. The organization of small, faith-based groups has in effect re-established the tradition of gender-segregated support groups, which existed even during the communist period, but they are now rooted in religious doctrine. Twenty-first century Bosnia is a space in which the revitalization of traditional religious practices has created a space for women to empower themselves, voice their opinions, and most importantly, become active agents in rebuilding their society.

---

11   Bringa, Tone: Being Muslim the Bosnian Way. Identity and Community in a Central Bosnian Village, Princeton/NJ: Princeton University Press, 1995.

Ulla Pape

12.   NGOs and HIV/AIDS in Russia. A Political Assessment

12.1. Introduction

Neglected for a long time, the HIV/AIDS epidemic in the Russian Federation has developed into a serious social and political problem. According to the United Nations Programme on HIV/AIDS (UNAIDS), Russia is currently facing the biggest HIV/AIDS epidemic in all of Europe with an estimated number of 940,000 people living with HIV.[1] An important factor in the unfolding of the epidemic in Russia has been the high number of injecting drug users (IDUs) among young people. Other specifically vulnerable groups include prison inmates, sex workers (SWs) and men, who have sex with men (MSM). In the past, the Russian government has been very slow in responding to the AIDS epidemic. For a long time, it has relied on testing rather than on broad prevention campaigns. Today, there are signs of a growing recognition that the epidemic's ongoing growth demands a scaled-up response. Russia's government has understood that HIV/AIDS forms a threat to social security and demographic development and, thus, is striving to develop new response strategies that also include collaboration with civil society.

Non-governmental organizations (NGOs), as the most prominent civil society actors, have been essential in the response to HIV/AIDS in Russia.[2] In many regions NGOs started the first prevention programmes throughout the 1990s when public response in this area was practically non-existent. One example for NGO activity today is the GLOBUS project, which is financed by the Global Fund and implemented by a consortium of five international and Russian NGOs. The development of civil society in post-Soviet Russia, however, has been far from unproblematic. Civic engagement and the formation of a participatory political culture can still be regarded as weak. Moreover, many Russian and foreign NGOs face difficulties from state authorities. The 2006 law on NGOs tightened the regulation concerning registration, programming and financing of NGOs, and is commonly understood as a sign that the government is seeking to extend its control over the non-governmental sector.[3] This overall political context creates a practical dilemma for NGOs in Russia as they need cooperation

---

1   UNAIDS: Eastern Europe and Central Asia. AIDS Epidemic Update 2007, March 2008, http://data. unaids.org/pub/Re port/2008/jc1529_epibriefs_eeurope_casia_en.pdf
2   Brown, Hannah: Russia's Blossoming Civil Society Holds the Key to HIV, in: The Lancet, 5 August 2006, Vol. 368, pp. 437–440.
3   International Centre for Not-for Profit Law (ICNL): Analysis of Russian NGO Law, 28 February 2006, http://www.icnl.org/knowledge/news/2006/02-28.htm

with state authorities on the local and national levels if their programmes want to be successful.

This chapter aims to analyse the role of NGOs in the fight against HIV/AIDS in the Russian Federation. Based on the global governance approach by L. Gordenker and T. G. Weiss, the particular power capabilities of NGOs in the response to HIV/AIDS in Russia will be investigated.[4] The chapter will thereby focus on the influence of NGOs on policy making in the field of HIV/AIDS and their collaboration with state institutions. The political interplay between NGOs and state institutions has been singled out as a field of particular interest as it shows both sides of a difficult – often paradoxical – relationship: on the one hand, civic initiative is still weakly developed and state institutions are often reluctant to cooperate with NGOs; on the other hand, however, state institutions do need NGO expertise and joint work with civil society in order to address effectively the HIV/AIDS epidemic in Russia. In short, the text will address the following research question: how did NGOs respond to the emerging HIV/AIDS epidemic in the Russian Federation, and to what extent have they been able to influence HIV/AIDS policy making over the past decade? As a case example, the activity of two AIDS-service NGOs in the region Tomsk will be discussed.

12.2. Background. Russia's HIV/AIDS Epidemic

The HIV/AIDS epidemic arrived in the region of Eastern Europe much later than in other parts of the world. Due to its political isolation, the first case of HIV infection in the then Soviet Union was only diagnosed in 1987. In 1995, the number of HIV infections in Russia was still as low as 1,000.[5] Twelve years later, the situation had changed dramatically. By the end of 2007, the number of registered HIV infections had risen to more than 400,000,[6] whereas the estimated number of unreported cases is believed to be much higher.

The rapid spread of HIV since the middle of the 1990s is predominantly driven by transmission via needle sharing among IDUs. To date, drug users remain the most vulnerable risk group. Furthermore, sexual transmission of HIV is on the rise, resulting in a growing number of women infected with HIV in Russia. The HIV/AIDS epidemic mainly affects young people. According to UNAIDS, 80% of the HIV positive are between four-

---

4   Gordenker, Leon / Weiss, Thomas G.: Pluralising Global Governance. Analytical Approaches and Dimensions, in: Third World Quarterly, 1995 (Vol. 16), No. 3, pp. 357–387, see also: Weiss, Thomas G. / Gordenker, Leon (eds): NGOs, the UN and Global Governance, London: Lynne Rienner Publishers, 1996.

5   Russian Federal AIDS Centre: Number of HIV-infected by 31 December 1995, http://www.hivrussia.org/stat/1995.shtml, accessed 22 May 2008.

6   Russian Federal AIDS Centre: Number of HIV-infected by 31 December 2007, http://www.hivrussia.org/stat/2007.shtml, accessed 22 May 2008.

teen and thirty years old.[7] Although efforts to combat HIV/AIDS have been intensified in recent years, the epidemic continues to grow, albeit not as fast as in the years 2000 and 2001. Today, HIV/AIDS affects more people in Russia than in any other country of Eastern Europe.

How could this alarming situation emerge? The underlying factors that enabled the spread of HIV/AIDS in Russia are complex. Next to a sharp increase in drug use, sexual behaviour has significantly changed after the end of the Soviet Union. There are no systematic sexual education programmes at schools which could provide reliable information on HIV/AIDS and prevent risky behaviour. Moreover, widespread stigma and discrimination against those groups of society which are most at risk, as for instance IDUs, SWs and MSM, contributed to the spread of HIV and made prevention efforts more difficult. Finally, the emergence of the HIV/AIDS crisis is closely linked to the transition process in Post-Soviet Russia, which seriously affected the health care system. In a period of decline and serious under-funding, Russian health care institutions have been unable to respond effectively to the emerging HIV/AIDS epidemic.

12.3. The Response to HIV/AIDS in Russia

The public response to HIV/AIDS in Russia has many shortcomings. First of all, the epidemiological surveillance of HIV infection is insufficient for tracking and understanding the epidemic in Russia. The statistics of the Federal AIDS Centre are based on officially registered cases of HIV infection. Systematic sentinel surveillance of high-risk groups, such as persons with tuberculosis or sexually transmitted infections, does not take place in many regions.[8] As a result, many experts believe that the official data do not reflect the actual epidemiological development of HIV/AIDS in Russia. Without credible official statistics, Russian health care officials and politicians are disinclined to view HIV/AIDS as a public health priority. Moreover, the lack of credibility of the Russian HIV/AIDS statistics makes it difficult to design concrete prevention programmes, particularly concerning difficult-to-reach high-risk groups.

The main state institution in the field of HIV/AIDS is the Federal AIDS Centre, which was already established during Soviet times, shortly after the first case of HIV infection had been diagnosed in 1987.[9] The Federal AIDS Centre is in charge of the epidemiological surveillance of HIV infection in the Russian Federation, as well as prevention, clinical diagnosis and medical care.[10] Directed by V.V. Pokrovsky, it consists of a network

7   UNAIDS: Global Summary of the AIDS Epidemic, December 2006, http://www.unaids.ru/en/HIV_data, accessed 27 May 2008.
8   Wallander, Celeste A.: Russian Politics and HIV/AIDS, in: Twigg, J. (ed.): HIV/AIDS in Russia and Eurasia, New York/NY: Palgrave Macmillan, 2006, pp. 33–55, p. 51.
9   Russian Federal AIDS Centre, http://www.hivrussia.org, accessed 24 May 2008.
10   Russian Federal AIDS Centre: Main Tasks of the Federal AIDS Centre, http://www.hivrussia.org, accessed 11 March 2008.

of federal, regional and municipal AIDS centres and is part of the Federal Service for Surveillance on Consumer Rights Protection and Human Wellbeing. The legal basis for the response to the epidemic is the 1995 Federal AIDS law, which guarantees free medical treatment for patients with HIV infection.[11]

During the 1990s, the Russian AIDS centres, as the health care system in general, suffered from structural under-funding. Due to lack of financial resources, the centres were unable to fulfil their tasks, particularly in the field of prevention. In most cases their work was restricted to diagnosis and registration of HIV infections in their specific region. Russian politicians to a large extent neglected the potential impact of the HIV/AIDS epidemic. This situation changed only after HIV/AIDS started to spread rapidly among young people after 1998.[12] The Russian government then realized that the epidemic required a political strategy. In 2003, president Putin first officially mentioned the problem of HIV/AIDS in Russia. After this political step, a number of new institutions were created with the aim of organizing and coordinating HIV/AIDS policy. At the political level, a Governmental Commission on HIV/AIDS was established in 2006. Chaired by Duma representative Michail Grishankov, it aims to coordinate federal and regional authorities in the implementation of key directions of the national HIV/AIDS policy. In addition, public funding of HIV/AIDS programmes was substantially increased over the past years.[13]

Although the Russian government has dedicated itself to the fight against HIV/AIDS,[14] its response to the epidemic still lacks a clear strategy. The importance of HIV/AIDS prevention has been recognized politically, but there is no consensus about *how* this could best be achieved. Acknowledged prevention strategies, as for instance harm reduction programmes, are not conducted on a scale that would allow them to have a real impact on the epidemic. Substitution therapy, which has been successfully applied in other countries of the region, is not approved in Russia. Moreover, attempts to introduce sexual education programmes in schools that could provide a basis for HIV/AIDS prevention for teenagers failed due to the opposition of the Russian Orthodox Church.[15] Those examples show that there is still a lot to be done before an effective response to the HIV/AIDS epidemic in Russia will be developed.

---

11 Federal AIDS Law 1995, in: Kodeks Russian Law Database, accessed 10 November 2006.
12 Russian Federal AIDS Centre: Statistics, http://www.hivrussia.org/stat/index.shtml, accessed 2 June 2008.
13 Federal Service for Surveillance on Consumer Rights Protection and Human Well-being: National Report of the Russian Federation, 30 March 2008, in: http://data.unaids.org/pub/Report/2008/russia_2008_country_progress_report_ru.pdf
14 Speech of Tatyana Golikova, Russian Minister of Health and Social Development, at the closing ceremony of the Second Eastern Europe and Central Asia Conference (EECAAC), 5 May 2008.
15 Kon, Igor: Better AIDS than sex education, in: Sandfort, Theo (ed.): The Sexual counter-revolution in Russia, London: Routledge, 2000, pp. 119–134.

12.4. Civil Society and HIV/AIDS

In the international context, the fight against HIV/AIDS has received much attention. Changing realities in a globalizing world and the threat of increasing global insecurity has led many country governments to support, at least partially, new governance arrangements in the area of international health, and in particular HIV/AIDS. For this emerging structure of global health politics the notion of 'global health governance' has been coined.[16] As a new field of international public policy, global health governance encompasses the formation of new organizations and programmes dealing with the response to the epidemic (UNAIDS),[17] international declarations (UNGASS),[18] funding mechanisms (Global Fund),[19] as well as guiding principles, strategies and implementation mechanisms.[20]

Within the emerging field of global health governance, civil society plays an important role. On the one hand, civil society actors, for instance NGOs, take an active part in the formulation and implementation of policies;[21] on the other hand, the involvement of civil society itself constitutes a principle in the regime of global health governance. According to the UNGASS Declaration of Commitment on HIV/AIDS, the

> full involvement and participation of civil society actors in the design, planning, implementation and evaluation of programs is crucial to the development of effective responses to the HIV/AIDS epidemic.[22]

As a main institution of global HIV/AIDS policy, UNAIDS acknowledges the essential role of civil society. It is believed that the active participation of NGOs makes prevention strategies more effective since NGOs can fulfil a bridge function to the most vulnerable and hard-to-reach populations and can thereby guarantee that HIV/AIDS prevention becomes rooted in local communities.

---

16 Hein, Wolfgang / Bartsch, Sonja / Kohlmorgen, Lars (eds): Global Health Governance and the Fight Against HIV/AIDS, Basingstoke: Palgrave Macmillan, 2007.
17 UNAIDS: Uniting the World Against AIDS, http://www.unaids.org/en, accessed 16 May 2008.
18 Declaration of Commitment on HIV/AIDS, United Nations General Assembly Special Session on HIV/AIDS, 25–27 June 2001, n. d., http://data.unaids.org/publications/irc-pub03/aidsdeclaration_en.pdf
19 The Global Fund to Fight AIDS, Tuberculosis and Malaria, http://www.theglobalfund.org
20 UNAIDS: Towards Universal Access, http://www.unaids.org/en/PolicyAndPractice/TowardsUniversalAccess/default.asp, accessed 12 May 2008.
21 Bartsch, Sonja / Kohlmorgen, Lars: The Role of Civil Society Organizations in Global Health Governance, in: Hein, Wolfgang / Bartsch, Sonja / Kohlmorgen, Lars (eds): Global Health Governance and the Fight Against HIV/AIDS, Basingstoke: Palgrave Macmillan, 2007, pp. 92–118, p. 99.
22 Declaration of Commitment on HIV/AIDS, United Nations General Assembly Special Session on HIV/AIDS, 25–27 June 2001, n. d., p. 14, http://data.unaids.org/publications/irc-pub03/aidsdeclaration_en.pdf

12.5. The Role of NGOs in the Response to HIV/AIDS in Russia

NGOs have been active in the response to HIV/AIDS from the beginning of the epidemic. Today, approximately 300 Russian NGOs are active on the local, regional and national levels.[23] The biggest and probably most well-known AIDS-service NGOs in Russia are the members of the NGO-consortium of the GLOBUS project, including the *Open Health Institute* (OHI), the *AIDS Foundation East-West* (AFEW), *Focus-Media, Population Services International* (PSI) and *AIDS Infoshare*. Those Moscow-based NGOs have a network of partner organizations in the Russian regions, with which they are conducting HIV/AIDS prevention programmes. AIDS-service NGOs in the regions vary from small initiatives to big grass-roots organizations with their own access to international donor organizations, for example the St. Petersburg NGO *Humanitarian Action*. Moreover, there are several networks of regional organizations which unite NGO activities on a federal level. One example is the *Russian Harm Reduction Network*, a partnership of NGOs promoting harm reduction strategies in Russia; another is the *Association of People Living with HIV/AIDS*, which unites self-help groups and advocacy organizations of HIV-positive people in Russia. The *Forum of AIDS-service NGOs in Russia*, finally, is an informal platform which aims to enhance the exchange and cooperation between Russian NGOs in the field of HIV/AIDS.

In order to analyse the role of AIDS-service NGOs and their influence on HIV/AIDS policy, we will turn to the global governance approach and take a closer look at their capability of achieving social change in the field of HIV/AIDS. According to Gordenker and Weiss, NGOs are concerned with gaining access and seeking influence in a globalizing world.[24] In contrast to traditional views on international relations, NGOs in this perception are regarded as having power capabilities and hence are able to play their roles, notwithstanding the differences between dominant states and small private actors.[25] NGOs can be understood as organizations which are private in their form and public in their purpose.[26] The heart of the matter, according to Gordenker and Weiss, is their advocacy of special interests of public importance, both in domestic politics and in intergovernmental arenas.[27]

Gordenker and Weiss propose studying NGO activity on the basis of the organizations' functions, including goals, relationships with other organizations and operating methods.[28] Regarding AIDS-service NGOs in Russia, we can observe three main

---

23 Twigg, J. / Skolnik, R.: Evaluation of the World Bank's Assistance in Responding to the AIDS Epidemic. Russia Case Study, Washington D.C.: The World Bank, 2005, p. 19.
24 Gordenker, Leon / Weiss, Thomas G.: Pluralising Global Governance. Analytical Approaches and Dimensions, in: Third World Quartely, 1995 (Vol. 16), No. 3, pp. 357–387, p. 358.
25 Ibid., p. 384.
26 Ibid., p. 364.
27 Ibid., p. 359.
28 Ibid., p. 382.

functions: (1) advocacy, (2) service provision and (3) empowerment. The first function of NGOs, advocacy, can be understood as the representation of interests from civil society, which otherwise are not been taken into account sufficiently.[29] From this perspective, NGOs act as agents for the marginalized and weak groups of society. Advocacy includes political lobbying in order to influence decision-making processes directly, as well as the mobilization of public opinion in order to prepare policy transformation and information campaigns with the aim of changing attitudes within society. The advocacy function is of particular importance in the field of HIV/AIDS policy in Russia as the epidemic mostly affects marginalized and disadvantaged groups that often do not have access to regular social and health care services. NGOs put the issue of HIV/AIDS on the political agenda by emphasizing that the epidemic is not a negligible phenomenon but affects the whole society, and particularly young people, who represent Russia's future. NGOs have, thus, played an important role in the policy shift towards the political recognition of HIV/AIDS in Russia. They have called attention to the epidemic and have campaigned for a comprehensive response strategy. The growing awareness within Russian society and among politicians demonstrates that AIDS-service NGOs achieved sustained success in their advocacy work.

The second function of NGOs includes the provision of services in the field of HIV/AIDS prevention, treatment, care and support. In fact, NGOs are today the most important service providers in this area. Since the early 1990s, NGOs have been conducting prevention programs as well as medical and social services. In many cases, NGOs are filling the gap left open by insufficient governmental health care services. An advantage of NGOs is that they enjoy trust within society and have access to difficult-to-reach high-risk groups, which are traditionally reluctant to approach state institutions for fear of being arrested by state authorities for participating in activities considered to be illegal. In comparison to public services, NGOs have a better understanding of the problems within society and are able to respond faster and more adequately. Moreover, NGOs are flexible and able to adopt new problem-solving strategies, which make their programmes more effective. In the area of HIV/AIDS prevention, NGOs have introduced new approaches and methods to Russia, including outreach, counselling and needle exchange, which consequently have also been adopted within the health care system. NGOs have, thus, been innovators in social policy. Furthermore, they have been successful in raising substantial funds for the fight against the HIV/AIDS epidemic in Russia by working together with international donor organizations. NGO programmes, financed by international donors, form the main part of the response to HIV/AIDS. In addition, high-scale funding of NGO programmes by the Global Fund led

29   Bartsch, Sonja / Lars Kohlmorgen: The Role of Civil Society Organizations in Global Health Governance, in: Hein, Wolfgang / Bartsch, Sonja / Kohlmorgen, Lars (eds): Global Health Governance and the Fight Against HIV/AIDS, Basingstoke: Palgrave Macmillan, 2007, pp. 92–118, p. 98.

to an increase in governmental funding. In 2006, the Russian government decided to raise its funds on HIV/AIDS and, at the same time, to refund the resources the Global Fund had spent in Russia. In this way, NGOs indirectly achieved an increase in government funding on HIV/AIDS.

Apart from advocacy and service provision, the third function of AIDS-service NGOs in Russia is empowerment, which can be understood as the process of gaining equal rights by those who are affected by the epidemic. In many cases, AIDS-service NGOs emerged from self-help initiatives. They often consist of people living with HIV (PLWH –People Living With HIV/AIDS), who aim to improve their living situation and advocate their rights.[30] The opportunity to exchange experiences with others and to get involved with an NGO helps them to retain control over the choices in their own lives.[31] In many regions, self-help groups and associations for PLWH were created to exchange experiences and provide mutual support. Their activity is closely related to advocacy, as the focus is on the protection of human rights. Many organizations, for instance the NGO *Positive Dialogue* in St. Petersburg, have their own legal consultations for people living with HIV/AIDS.[32] Self-help organizations of PLWH played a crucial role in ensuring access to medical treatment, including antiretroviral therapy (ART). It is partly due to those NGOs that access to ART has been expanded to all regions of Russia.

Assessing the role of AIDS-service NGOs and their functions of advocacy, service-provision and empowerment, we can conclude that they indeed posses specific power capabilities in the response to HIV/AIDS. Their strengths include the capability to raise funds, to develop services that respond to the needs of the population, to transfer know-how regarding new approaches and methods in social work, to develop and apply expertise, and to enable people to assert their rights.

12.6. The Example of Tomsk

In order to better understand the role of NGOs in HIV/AIDS prevention in Russia, we will take a closer look at two AIDS-service NGOs in the West Siberian region Tomsk. With a HIV prevalence of 97.2 per 100,000 members of the population, Tomsk is considered to be a region with middle HIV prevalence in the Russian Federation.[33] The region distinguishes itself by the active involvement of civil society in the field of HIV/AIDS. The two main AIDS-service NGOs are *Siberian AIDS Aid* and *Tomsk Anti SPID*.

---

30   Bartsch, Sonja / Kohlmorgen, Lars: The Role of Civil Society Organizations in Global Health Governance, in: Hein, Wolfgang / Bartsch, Sonja / Kohlmorgen, Lars (eds): Global Health Governance and the Fight Against HIV/AIDS, Basingstoke: Palgrave Macmillan, 2007, pp. 92–118.
31   Ibid., p. 100.
32   Positive Dialogue, http://www.aidsinfo.spb.ru, accessed 28 May 2008.
33   Kmietowicz, Zosia: Tomsk – A Glimpse of one Russian Region's Experience with HIV/AIDS, in: British Medical Journal, 20 May 2006; 332 (7551): 1176.

The Regional Charitable Fund *Siberian AIDS Aid* was founded as a grass-roots organization in December 1995. It owes its existence to the pioneering spirit and assertiveness of its two founders, who started the NGO as a private project. Today, *Siberian AIDS Aid* has developed into a professional AIDS-service organization with seven staff members and about fifty volunteers. The NGO aims

> to realise the right of every person to receive reliable and up-to-date information concerning sexually transmitted diseases, including HIV/AIDS, drug addiction and human rights in the field of public health.[34]

In the 1990s, *Siberian AIDS Aid* was the first organization that started HIV/AIDS prevention programmes in Tomsk region. With no state programmes on HIV/AIDS existing at that time, the NGO thus responded to a basic information need among the population. Today, *Siberian AIDS Aid* predominantly focuses on young people by organizing information and awareness-raising campaigns in schools, universities and youth clubs. Working with volunteers is very effective in Tomsk as the student city has a very young and active population. In addition to its general volunteer programme for young people, *Siberian AIDS Aid* runs a special programme for MSM. On the regional and local level, the NGO cooperates with other NGOs as well as with state institutions such as the Municipal Department of Education and the Department of Youth Policy, Physical Culture and Sport of Tomsk Region. On the federal level, *Siberian AIDS Aid* is in close contact with the NGO consortium of the GLOBUS project, which funds part of its programmes.

In contrast to the grass-roots NGO *Siberian AIDS Aid*, the second AIDS-service organization of the region, *Tomsk Anti SPID*, was established in the year 2000 with active involvement from the Regional AIDS Centre and can thus be regarded as a government-organized non-governmental organization. According to its profile, the organization has the goal of 'preventing HIV/AIDS and drug use in Tomsk region by information provision and services.'[35] *Tomsk Anti SPID* focuses on secondary HIV/AIDS prevention and programmes for high-risks groups, such as IDUs and SWs. A team of medical doctors, psychologists and social workers offers services such as testing for HIV and other sexually transmitted infections, pre- and post-test counselling and psychological support. The NGO is working with a network of trusted medical specialists in Tomsk, who are ready to treat its clients. Moreover, *Tomsk Anti SPID* is in contact with the drug rehabilitation centre and the tuberculosis clinic in the city, where clients can decide to enrol for treatment. The organization also conducts outreach work, which includes the provision of condoms and health information to drug users and sex workers on the street or at meeting places. One of the biggest achievements of *Tomsk Anti SPID* is the harm reduction programme, which provides sterile equipment for IDUs as

---

34 Siberian AIDS Aid, http://www.aids.tomsk.ru, accessed 12 May 2008.
35 Tomsk Anti Spid, http://aids.xemi.info, accessed 14 May 2008.

well as condoms and information on health issues. The programme in Tomsk is one of the first in Russia and can be regarded as a pioneer project. A notable strength of the NGO is the contact with and access to difficult-to-reach high-risk groups such as IDUs and SWs, who are often disinclined to approach a state institution like the AIDS Centre or a regular clinic. *Tomsk Anti SPID* sees its role as a mediator between its clients and the health care system. The organizational link with the Regional AIDS Centre helps *Tomsk Anti SPID* in the realization of its programmes by facilitating close cooperation with medical institutions and case management. Due to this institutional backing, the NGO is able to take up difficult issues such as harm reduction, to develop social services and to influence social policy in the region from the bottom up.

Both examples show that AIDS-service NGOs establish close links with state institutions on a regional level such as the AIDS centre and the regional and municipal administration. This cooperation enables them to further develop their services and to assert their influence on the planning of HIV/AIDS response strategies in the region. NGOs are valued because of their expertise, their innovative working style and their access to both high-risk groups and youth in general. Referring to Gordenker and Weiss, their power capabilities lie in the connection of advocacy, service provision and empowerment. The main challenge for the future remains the acquisition of state funding for AIDS-service NGOs and the political recognition of those programmes that are not easily incorporated into the public response strategy, for instance harm reduction and HIV/AIDS prevention programmes for MSM.

12.7. Conclusions. Power and Limits of NGOs

NGOs are indeed key players in the fight against HIV/AIDS in Russia. They were the first to understand the urgency of the epidemic and to take up action. In many regions in Russia, NGOs played a pioneering role in starting HIV/AIDS prevention and care programs. NGOs were also the first to address the most vulnerable and marginalized groups of society, which are often excluded from government health services and exposed to discrimination and stigma. NGOs understood that services for those high-risk groups are not only a moral imperative, but also an essential precondition to stem the HIV/AIDS epidemic in general.

The examples of the organizations *Siberian AIDS Aid* and *Tomsk Anti SPID* show, which strategies NGOs are using to assert influence on HIV/AIDS policy. Both organizations have made an important contribution to the fight against HIV/AIDS, by combining advocacy, service provision and empowerment. The NGO *Tomsk Anti SPID* is successful in prevention programs, addressing vulnerable groups as IDUs and SWs. *Siberian AIDS Aid*, on the other hand, focuses on prevention and harm reduction programs for a broader public and has been able to reach many young people in the region. In comparison to government services, both NGOs have the advantage that they can address the needs of society more directly. The two NGOs *Siberian AIDS Aid* and *Tomsk Anti SPID* conduct essential services in the field of HIV/AIDS, but also advocate for an improvement of the response to the epidemic in general. Moreover, they raise funds from donor organizations, which can directly be used for projects on the ground. Finally, they are able to involve volunteers in their projects, thereby increasing the coverage and impact of their activities.

However, AIDS-service NGOs should not be misunderstood as a mere substitute for government action. In the current political context of Russia, they run the risk of being instrumentalized and reduced to the role of service providers, which undermines their strength in advocating for the needs and rights of vulnerable groups of society. Clarifying roles and forms of cooperation between the state and the NGO sector is therefore essential for the realization of a successful and comprehensive HIV/AIDS policy in Russia.

Thijs Rommens

13. The Impact of the European Neighbourhood Policy on Democratization in the South Caucasus

13.1. Introduction

The theorem generally assumed in research on EU democracy promotion focuses on the use of conditionality based on the attractiveness of EU membership to potential candidate countries. With the European Neighbourhood Policy (ENP) the EU has sent a clear message to countries such as Ukraine and Georgia that membership is no longer an option. This severely limits the further use of conditionality and puts into question the prevalent theories on democracy promotion by the EU. However, this does not mean that there is no room for other ways and mechanisms through which the ENP could lead to democratization. These other prospects demand another research agenda and a broadening of the number of levels and actors involved. This chapter aims to contribute to this by focusing on the role of civil society organizations and their use of the ENP in order to push for democratization. The cases studied here are Azerbaijan and Georgia; both regimes are balancing between authoritarianism and democratizing tendencies. Local civil society organizations are often pushing for the latter and in this chapter their reliance on the framework of the ENP to do so is examined. This can be fit in with the broader research on international democracy promotion.

Initial literature on democratization offered a rather optimistic outlook based on a procedural concept of democratization.[1] The research agenda has been broadened and other dimensions, such as a free market, the rule of law and civil society, have come to the fore. Civil society plays a vital role in this more comprehensive view on democratization in that it could potentially serve as a bridge between politics and society at large. In this capacity, civil society bundles and expresses interests, demands and values in a bottom-up manner independently of the state. The existence of a robust and functioning civil society strengthens both the performance and credibility of the government and helps to create a sustainable democracy. Civil society provides the government with expertise on problems, informs it of public expectations and needs, and, if tapped, could boost the government's legitimacy. Civil society and democracy are thus intertwined to a great extent. The former requires a democratic political system guaranteeing civic freedoms; at the same time, the strength of a democ-

---

1   Zakaria, Fareed: The future of freedom, illiberal democracy at home and abroad, London: W.W. Norton and Company, 2004, p. 17.

racy is partly defined by the level of civil society.[2] This symbiotic existence reflects the situation in established democracies. The key to democratization is thus to foster this kind of interaction.

The success of international democratization assistance has paradoxically triggered a backlash against democracy promotion[3] and an increasing number of authoritarian leaders have criticized international interference in national politics. The original positive assessment of the impact of international actors on democratization has given way to a less clear-cut picture. The impact of international actors has been assumed, but rarely proven.[4] Sceptics argue that international actors are only of secondary importance and that regime change is primarily a dynamic process that is internally motivated. A mere dichotomous analysis does not reflect the reality of the complex, dynamic process of interaction between international factors and domestic elements.

More subtle forms of influencing democratization from the outside that take into account both international and domestic elements have been brought to the fore by researchers and policymakers. Different theoretical models have emerged on the topic of external influence on democratization. W. Jacoby[5] offers an overview of these models. One mode is 'inspiration', in which ideas flow from the outside to the inside, a method often used in the post-communist world. The idea behind it is that domestic reformers look abroad to find best practices and try to emulate experiences from other countries. Another mode is 'substitution', whereby external actors attempt to promote and implement their programme directly regardless of the internal preferences or balance of power. A third method, called the 'coalition' mode, falls between these two extremes and leaves an active role for both the inside and outside actors. In this approach outsiders strive to influence the choices of existing domestic actors with whom they can form a coalition. The exact mechanisms through which this external support is channelled are diverse and cover more than mere subsidies and financial backing. By actively interfering in the domestic political sphere, the external actor can alter time horizons and incentives and thus improve the conditions for changes it favours. This mode is arguably the least easy to see with the naked eye, yet it has become the most prominent mode of international democracy promotion. It implies that when studying democratization, one needs to take into account both domestic and international actors as well as cooperation between insiders and outsiders.

---

2   Raik, Kristi: Promoting democracy through civil society, CEPS Working Document, 2006, No. 237, p. 4.
3   Carothers, Thomas: The backlash against democracy promotion, in: Foreign Affairs, 2006, (Vol. 85), No. 2, pp. 55–68.
4   Pridham, Geoffrey: Building democracy? The international dimension of democratisation in Eastern Europe, London: Leicester University Press, 1997, p. 9.
5   Jacoby, Wade: Inspiration, Coalition, and substitution, external influences on postcommunist transformation, in: World Politics, 2006 (Vol. 58), No. 4, pp. 623–651.

In the ENP, the golden carrot of membership is not an option, which makes the use of conditionality less implementable. Because the EU has less leverage over the partner countries, it will have to come up with other ways of promoting democratization. The current shift of attention away from conditionality will deeply affect the future of the EU's democracy promotion and assistance. The use of conditionality is closely linked to the logic of consequence; actors are incited to act according to the wishes of another actor via the linking of compliance to rewards. The more complex and fundamental logic of appropriateness complements this means of democratization; it asserts that actors tend to conform to rules of appropriate behaviour. Its logic is rooted in the assumptions of social constructivism. Actors do not merely act in their own interest, but they are also motivated by social interaction, which they use to construct their identity.[6] Socialization is the key process here: actors who are surrounded by the values and norms of democracy can internalize these after a certain amount of time.

As conditionality plays a lesser role in the ENP, the potential importance for the logic of appropriateness has increased. This shift in rationale and the potential interaction between the logic of appropriateness and of consequence constitute the focus of this chapter. On the face of it, democracy promotion does not seem to have the same prospects as it had during the earlier process of enlargement. This does not mean however that other mechanisms could not be at work. There is room for other means and mechanisms to influence the effectiveness of democracy promotion in the setting of the ENP. By expanding the traditional framework of analysis this contribution explores these alternatives. Returning to the theory on democracy promotion mentioned above: is the ENP a successful example of the coalition approach?

13.2. Theoretical Approach

The concept of rhetorical action coined by Frank Schimmelfennig[7] is applied in this research and adapted to fit the specific case. Schimmelfennig developed the theory in the context of the EU and NATO enlargements: why did Western European states agree to these enlargements? He starts his analysis by comparing the preferences of the Western European states at the beginning of the negotiation process with the eventual outcome of the accession talks. The outcome of the process does not match the initial predictions based on the interests of the member states. The enlargement preferences and initial enlargement decision-making process correspond to rationalist expectations (logic of consequence), which attribute actor preferences and behaviour

---

6   Risse, Thomas: 'Let's argue!' Communicative action in world politics, in: International Organization, 2000 (Vol. 54), No. 1, pp. 1–39.

7   Schimmelfennig, Frank: The community trap. Liberal norms, rhetorical action, and the eastern enlargement of the EU in International Organization, 2001 (Vol. 55), No. 1, pp. 47–80.

as well as collective outcomes to egoistic calculations of material interest and differ-
ential bargaining power. The outcome of the process, however, follows the rationale
of sociological institutionalism (logic of appropriateness), which explains why the two
organizations finally admitted new member states from Central and Eastern Europe
and the reasons for their selection. Yet, this theory is unable to tell us how this outcome was produced. The analytical problem to be solved is to explain how a process initially determined by egoistic preferences and strategic action resulted in a rule-
conforming outcome.

Schimmelfennig brings in the mechanism of rhetorical action as the causal link
between the egoistic point of departure and the rule-based final outcome. Rhetorical
action draws on a strategic conception of rules that combines a social, ideational ontol-
ogy with the assumption of rational action. It postulates that social actors use and
exchange arguments based on identities, values and norms institutionalized in their
environment to defend their political claims and persuade their opponents and their
audience to accept these claims and to act accordingly.[8] In this research we transplant
and adapt Schimmelfennig's mechanism to the context of the ENP and its potential
for internal democratization in the three Caucasus Republics.

As mentioned above, in case of the ENP, official documents explicitly mention
shared values as the number one priority and the neighbouring countries are also
tied to these principles. Because the agreements between the EU and the countries
do not only touch upon material or institutional aspects, but also upon norms and
values, rhetorical action can be applied. The commitments made between national
governments and the EU serve as a potential source to refer to, which opens up the
possibility for the use of this mechanism in our analysis.

The crucial divergence from the original theory rests in the actors involved. Whereas
Schimmelfennig's paradigm covers relations between member states and applicants,
the focus here is on NGOs and their eventual use of commitments made in the ENP.
The declared pledge to strengthen democracy formulated in the ENP Action Plans for
external use can resonate in domestic politics. It may not be in the interest of auto-
cratic regimes to do so themselves, but there is a possibility that NGOs will take up
that promise and usher it into the domestic political arena. NGOs working on democracy could refer to the ENP to strengthen their own position. In this setting, rhetorical
action is situated between the government and the NGOs.

---

8   Schimmelfennig, Frank: The EU, NATO and the integration of Europe. Rules and rhetoric,
     Cambridge: Cambridge University Press, 2003, p. 193.

13.3. The EU as Democracy Promoter

The EU has been an organization for and of democratic states from the outset, but it did not make political conditionality with respect to democracy a cornerstone of its external relations until Greece, Spain and Portugal applied for membership in the 1970s. The successful democratic consolidation of these countries seemed to confirm the pivotal role that the EU can play in promoting democracy. The fall of communism would eventually provide a rich opportunity to test this hypothesis. Every policy initiative since, such as PHARE or the Association Agreements, has contained elements of conditionality and democratization. This was formalized during the accession talks when democratic norms were explicitly enshrined in the Copenhagen criteria. At the end of the process, various post-communist countries joined the EU and their political systems were classified as consolidated democracies. This apparent success story could be harder for the EU to achieve in the future.[9]

In the 2004 ENP Strategy Paper, 'commitment to specific actions which confirm or reinforce adherence to shared values'[10] is cited as the first of two priority areas for the ENP. Further on in the text these values are extolled as strengthening not only democracy, but also respect for human rights, support for the development of civil society, cooperation with the International Criminal Court and cooperation with the EU's external actions.[11] Democratization thus has top billing, but in order for it to take effect, it has to trickle down to the Country Reports and Action Plans, which serve as basis for actual policy-making. In the Country Reports, the emphasis is on legislative reform and liberalization; the judicial and economic sectors dominate the texts. However, the Reports also contain two fairly extensive sections on democracy and human rights that appear fairly direct and concrete. Although these Commission-produced Reports served as a starting point for the Action Plans, they seem to lack the rigour and details of the initial Reports, in which value gaps were identified.[12] The Action Plan for Georgia, for example, mentions eight priority areas and only lists democratization as a complementary action.[13] This illustrates that democratization has not been translated into concrete terms on the highest level of policy-making.

In addition, the intergovernmental nature of the negotiations of the Action Plans has also served to shut out NGOs and civil society in general. Not only does this exclusionary approach mean a loss of potential civil society involvement, but it contradicts the stated aims of the ENP as mentioned above to support the development of civil

---

9   Kubicek, Paul J.: The European Union and democratization, London: Routledge, 2003, p. 10.
10   European Commission: Communication from the Commission. European Neighbourhood Policy. Strategy Paper, COM (2004) 373 final, 12 May 2004, p. 9.
11   Ibid., p. 13.
12   Bosse, Giselle: Values in the EU's Neighbourhood Policy, in: European Political Economy Review, 2007, No. 7, pp. 38–62.
13   European Commission: EU/Georgia Action Plan, November 2006.

society. After fierce protesting from civil society organizations, the EU has made efforts to include civil society in the ENP in a more active way. Meetings between EU officials and NGO representatives are organized in ENP countries to strengthen ties and civil society representatives were invited to the European Commission ENP conference in September 2007.[14] Although these are laudable first steps to improve dialogue, civil society remains a secondary actor in the mainly bilateral ENP process.

13.4. Tentative Results

Literature on the role of civil society in post-communist societies often stresses its relative weakness compared to other regions. The legacy of Soviet times still influences the image of civil society organizations. During the communist era, autonomous organizations were not only repressed, but also supplanted by state-run counterparts. In response to this, an extensive network of personal relations and informal connections developed. Today's relatively less vibrant civil society stems in part from disappointment; people who were active in promoting democracy before the fall have been disheartened by the sometimes sobering events of the first post-communist years.[15]

Besides the historical lack of trust in NGOs, there are also a number of flaws and issues that originate from within civil society itself. The ideal of civil society as an entity working from the bottom up to communicate the larger population's needs to the political field does not seem to fit the situation in the South Caucasus. Organizations tend to be professionally organized rather than more or less organically emerging from societal needs. Many NGOs seem more interested in defending the interests of their employees instead of furthering the common good of society. Moreover, because they tend to be personality-driven rather than issue-driven, NGOs are often dependent on the activities of one or several key figures. Another issue is their substantial dependence on donors; organizations often scramble in competition with other NGOs for income instead of focussing on implementing policies.[16] However, many NGOs conduct useful work and address important problems, even if their efforts are often not visible to the public. Their good deeds do not receive the same degree of media attention as cases involving misappropriated funds or other scandals.

Civil society organizations do not operate in a political vacuum and as relatively new actors, they have to position themselves in order to get heard and gain credibility. In the case of the South Caucasus, this is not so easy to achieve because certain security-related topics tend to dominate the political debate. This leaves little room

---

14   Reflections from Civil Society representatives, European Commission ENP Conference, 3 September 2007, p. 7.
15   Howard, Marc M.: The weakness of post communist civil society, in: Journal of Democracy, 2002 (Vol. 13), No. 1, pp. 157–169.
16   Interview with Böll Stiftung representative, November 2007.

for organizations to challenge certain societal problems without being discredited by political opponents. In Georgia, inequality and poverty are rising and are thus becoming more pressing issues; however, there are fewer civil society organizations working on these topics than one would expect. Organizations that do tackle these issues have been branded as communist, a label that is still negatively associated with Russian rule. In a country that has had tense relations with Russia over the last several years, joining an organization with communist overtones could ruin one's status and sever links to authorities.[17] In Armenia and Azerbaijan, the NGOs' room for manoeuvre is similarly squeezed by the Nagorno-Karabakh conflict.

International linkages between internal civil society and international actors have been thriving in the region since the fall of communism. The most active organizations were from the US, such as the Soros Foundation and the International Republican Institute, German foundations and international organizations such as the UN and the OSCE.

These programmes have witnessed different outcomes in the different countries. In Azerbaijan, there is not much room for civil society to participate in politics and the government is also not inclined to increase this. The lack of a free press and of an independent judicial branch makes it difficult for civil society to make itself heard and create a solid basis for action.[18] In spite of its international links, civil society in Azerbaijan plays a relatively small role, which shows that national factors have to be taken into account and that mere inspiration will not produce the desired outcome.

Georgia is widely touted as a textbook example of a successful civil society that has been able to induce political change. The Rose Revolution and Saakashvili's rise to power were greatly supported by a large number of NGOs. Linkages between local actors such as NGOs, political parties and individuals from Georgia and international (mainly US) actors were plentiful. Once the Shevardnadze regime fell, opposition forces assumed power and a substantial number of people from civil society took up positions in the new government.

The main question in this instance is if it is appropriate for civil society to actually take political power. Assuming office tends to undermine its credibility, because in retrospect, it can appear that civil society members merely used NGOs to promote their own political agendas, which is antithetical to the concept of civil society. And when civil society members join the government, the public is robbed of key actors. The extensive link to the US that some NGOs have also creates grounds for opponents to discredit them as puppets controlled by America. The Georgian case also is an example of 'where you stand is where you sit' in that the same people who opposed strong

---

17   Interview with Georgian NGO staff member, November 2007.
18   United States Agency for International Development: 2006 NGO Sustainability Index for Central and Eastern Europe and Eurasia, Washington D. C.: USAID, 2007.

centralization did not change the status quo once they came to power.[19] International empowerment of civil society can thus lead to bringing down regimes, but it is not self-evident that it automatically leads to further democratization.

The EU is a relative latecomer on the democracy promotion scene in the South Caucasus. It is only since the beginning of 2008 that an EU delegation has been active in all three countries. The main instrument the EU uses to encourage civil society and democratization is the European Instrument for Democracy and Human Rights (EIDHR), whose second general objective (out of five) is the strengthening of civil society. Through dedicated members of staff at the local delegations, the EU supports a number of projects run by NGOs. In Georgia about thirty projects were going on in 2007 for a total sum of one million euro.[20] The contacts between the EU and civil society have increased since the introduction of the ENP. A first conference on the role of civil society was organized in June 2007 with officials from the EU Commission and the Delegation as well as members from Georgian NGOs attending. In recent years, the EU has managed to foster links with Georgian civil society.

Have the EU and the ENP managed to attract the attention of local civil society apart from being a source of funding? Among the general public, the EU is neither considered the most important international actor nor the ENP the most pressing issue. In Georgia, membership in NATO is priority number one on the foreign policy agenda and the US rather than the EU is seen the main guarantor against possible Russian aggression. Azerbaijan conducts a multi-vector foreign policy and has not openly applied for EU membership. With regards to human rights and civil society, the Council of Europe has the most significant leverage.

The relatively meagre attention paid to the ENP extends to civil society. A small number of domestic NGOs is working on the topic. This can be explained by a number of factors already touched upon. The vagueness of the programme makes benchmarking and monitoring difficult. The vagueness of the European level is also noticeable on the domestic level. The Georgian government worked out a detailed matrix covering all necessary actions, but this was rejected as too detailed and a working paper of eight pages replaced it. NGOs also do not have much experience in dealing with the EU, as it has only recently become involved in democracy promotion. The multilevel constitution of the ENP ads an EU-level, complicating things for NGOs that still struggle to survive just on the national level.

This rather bleak outlook for the chances for the ENP to have any impact at all on democratization in the region has to be tempered. International actors such as the Open Society Institute and the Böll Stiftung have been actively supporting ENP monitoring initiatives. Both in Azerbaijan as in Georgia consortia have come into existence

---

19   Interview with EU Delegation member, Tbilisi, November 2007.
20   Interview with EU Delegation member, Tbilisi, November 2007.

which bring local civil society organizations and international organizations together to observe the implementation of the ENP. During the different stages of drafting, signing and implementing the Action Plan a number of reports and recommendations were published.[21] Through regular follow-ups of the topic, these organizations try to get the voice of civil society heard. In Georgia some seventy civil society organizations produced a list of recommendations for the Georgian government in 2005 with support from Open Society, Heinrich Böll Stiftung and the Eurasia Foundation. Although this list did not directly materialize into formal involvement of civil society in the ENP Action Plan policy drafting, it raised interest in the subject and promoted a feeling of responsibility. The aims set for the future of the organization are further cooperation between civil society, the political elite, the media and other interest groups through intensifying debates and discussions about the ENP. A similar initiative has been developed in Azerbaijan. The National Committee for European Integration has been set up under the auspices of Open Society. The Committee brings together fifty-four organizations, scholars, business representatives and journalists and aims to raise awareness through campaigning, policy papers and civic participation.[22]

13.5. Future Prospects

This dynamic is very interesting because it furnishes proof of an even more complex setup. Not only do we have international linkages between the EU and local civil society, but international NGOs are also involved. Local NGOs are now acting upon the agreements between national governments and the EU on democratization because international NGOs have encouraged them to do so. This preliminary conclusion leads us to the question of whether this will turn into a stable nexus of actors that will succeed in creating a sustainable dynamic concerning the implementation of democratization as envisioned by the ENP.

The direct impact of the ENP on democratization in the republics of the South Caucasus may be limited, but there are more complex and oblique effects which could strengthen democratization in a more indirect way. Through changes in power relations and the introduction of the rhetoric of democratization the ENP opens up room for the use of rhetorical action. Combined with the international dimension of emerging networks around the ENP a more comprehensive assessment of the potential for democratization is formulated.

This evaluation could be used by the EU as a starting point for further action strengthening democracy in the region. As the traditional mechanism of conditionality

---

21   Open Society Georgia Foundation / For Transparency of Public Finances: Georgia and the European Neighbourhood Policy perspectives and challenges, Tbilisi, 2007.
22   Azerbaijan National Committee for European Integration: About Committee, http://www.aamik. az/ts_gen/eng/komite_haqqinda.htm, accessed 13 July 2008.

no longer applies, tapping into this potential could partly make up for this loss. If the EU could develop a coherent strategy to include these networks in ENP monitoring and policy drafting it could continue to promote democracy and strengthen its image of being a soft power.

About the Authors

Elitsa Dimitrova is a research fellow at the Center for Population Studies, which is part of the Bulgarian Academy of Sciences.

Sanin Hasibovic, MA, is a research associate at the Department of Political Science, University of Vienna, Austria.

Emira Ibrahimpasic is a Ph.D. candidate at the Department of Anthropology, University of New Mexico, USA.

Ingi Iusmen is a Ph.D. student at the University of Strathclyde – Department of Government, Glasgow, Great Britain.

Noemi Kakucs is currently Programme Coordinator at the Department of Political Science and a junior researcher at the Department of Gender Studies, Central European University, Budapest, Hungary.

Robert Kulpa is a Ph.D. student at Birkbeck College, London, Great Britain.

Manja Nickel, MA, is a research associate at the Department of Political Science, University of Vienna, Austria.

Ulla Pape is a Ph.D. student in the Department of International Relations and International Organisation, University of Groningen, The Netherlands.

Raluca Prelipceanu is a Ph.D. student at the Sorbonne Centre for Economics (CES), University of Paris, 1 Pantheon Sorbonne, France.

Thijs Rommens is a research fellow and teaching assistant at the Institute for International and European Policy, University of Leuven, Belgium.

Robert Sata is a postdoctoral research fellow at the Department of Political Science, Central European University, Budapest, Hungary.

Suhal Semsit is a research assistant and Ph.D. candidate at the Department of EU Studies, Institute of Social Sciences, Dokuz Eylül University, Turkey.

Marlene Spoerri is a Ph.D. candidate at the University of Amsterdam, The Netherlands.

Anna Wylegała is a Ph.D. student at the Graduate School for Social Research, Warsaw, Poland.

Series Subscription

Please enter my subscription to the series *Changing Europe*, ISSN 1863-8716, as follows:

starting with
- ❏ volume # 1
- ❏ volume # ___
  - ❏ please also include the following volumes: #___, ___, ___, ___, ___, ___,

- ❏ the next volume being published
  - ❏ please also include the following volumes: #___, ___, ___, ___, ___, ___,

- ❏ 1 copy per volume   OR   ❏ ___ copies per volume

Subscription within Germany:

You will receive every volume at 1st publication at the regular bookseller's price – incl. s & h and VAT.

Payment:
- ❏ Please bill me for every volume.
- ❏ Lastschriftverfahren: Ich/wir ermächtige(n) Sie hiermit widerruflich, den Rechnungsbetrag je Band von meinem/unserem folgendem Konto einzuziehen.

Kontoinhaber: _____ Kreditinstitut: _____

Kontonummer: _____ Bankleitzahl: _____

International Subscription:

Payment (incl. s & h and VAT) in advance for
- ❏ 10 volumes/copies (€ 319.80)   ❏ 20 volumes/copies (€ 599.80)
- ❏ 40 volumes/copies (€ 1,099.80)

Please send my books to:

NAME_____ DEPARTMENT_____
ADDRESS _____
POST/ZIP CODE_____ COUNTRY _____
TELEPHONE _____ EMAIL_____

date/signature_____

A hint for librarians in the former Soviet Union: Your academic library might be eligible to receive free-of-cost scholarly literature from Germany via the German Research Foundation. For Russian-language information on this program, see
     http://www.dfg.de/forschungsfoerderung/formulare/download/12_54.pdf.

Please fax to: **0511 / 262 2201 (+49 511 262 2201)**
or mail to: *ibidem*-Verlag, Julius-Leber-Weg 11, D-30457 Hannover, Germany
or send an e-mail: ibidem@ibidem-verlag.de

ibidem-Verlag

Melchiorstr. 15

D-70439 Stuttgart

info@ibidem-verlag.de

www.ibidem-verlag.de
www.ibidem.eu
www.edition-noema.de
www.autorenbetreuung.de